THE MIXED-BREED DOG

Phyllis DeGioia

The Mixed-Breed Dog

Project Team
Editor: Stephanie Fornino and Heather Russell-Revesz
Copy Editor: Joann Woy
Design: Stephanie Krautheim
Series Design: Stephanie Krautheim and Mada Design
Series Originator: Dominique De Vito

T.F.H. Publications
President/CEO: Glen S. Axelrod
Executive Vice President: Mark E. Johnson
Publisher: Christopher T. Reggio
Production Manager: Kathy Bontz

T.F.H. Publications, Inc.
One TFH Plaza
Third and Union Avenues
Neptune City, NJ 07753

Printed and bound in China
07 08 09 10 1 3 5 7 9 8 6 4 2
Library of Congress Cataloging-in-Publication Data
DeGioia, Phyllis.
  The mixed-breed dog / Phyllis DeGioia.
     p. cm.
  Includes index.
  ISBN 978-0-7938-3675-8 (alk. paper)
  1. Mutts (Dogs) I. Title.
  SF427.D384 2007
  636.7'1--dc22
                    2007002622

This book has been published with the intent to provide accurate and authoritative information in regard to the subject matter within. While every precaution has been taken in preparation of this book, the author and publisher expressly disclaim responsibility for any errors, omissions, or adverse effects arising from the use or application of the information contained herein. The techniques and suggestions are used at the reader's discretion and are not to be considered a substitute for veterinary care. If you suspect a medical problem consult your veterinarian.

The Leader In Responsible Animal Care For Over 50 Years.™
www.tfh.com

TABLE OF CONTENTS

HISTORY

of the Mixed Breed

As George Bernard Shaw put it, "I like a bit of mongrel myself, whether it's in a man or a dog; they're the best for every day." Mixed breeds are often referred to as mutts, Heinz 57s, mongrels, curs, random-bred, hybrids, pariahs, and crossbreeds. The variety of titles is appropriate, given how unique each dog is. However, there are some useful terms dog fanciers use to designate certain types of non-purebred dogs. *Mixed-breed* dogs most often refer to dogs whose parents were mixes of other breeds, but often have a recognizable "type" in them, such as Shepherd or Terrier. Usually the mating is unplanned or unintentional. *Crossbreeds* usually refer to dogs who had two purebred parents of different breeds. The mating for these types of dogs is usually planned, or "selectively bred." (You'll sometimes hear these dogs referred to as "designer dogs.") *Hybrids* most often refer to the offspring between two different species. Then there are the *pariah* dogs—feral dogs who live on the fringes of human settlements. For the purposes of this book, "mixed breed" will refer to all types of non-purebred dogs kept as pets (unless otherwise indicated).

Whether you have a dog whose heritage is a colorful patchwork of many different breeds, an unknown commodity, or a planned combination of two breeds, your mix is bound to be "top dog" in your eyes.

A LONG, LONG TIME AGO

A few millennia ago, dogs as we know them did not exist. Most scientists believe that what we call dogs today—*Canis lupus familiaris*—descended from wolves. In fact, domesticated dogs are members of the family *Canidae*, which also

Dogs and wolves are members of the same scientific family, Canidae.

Canaan Dogs

The current Canaan Dog has been developed from redomesticated, ancient Pariah Dog stock (wild or feral dogs who tend to live near humans) in Palestine. Canaans have a medium-sized, square body. The Canaan's head is wedge-shaped with prick ears, and he has a bushy tail that curls over the back when excited. The double coat is straight, harsh, and lies flat, and there are a lot of coat colors ranging from white to black and most colors in between. Even though he looks like a mixed-breed to many people, the Canaan Dog is recognized by the American Kennel Club (AKC).

includes wolves, coyotes, and jackals. All these canine types have the same number of chromosomes, which means if a dog mates with a wolf, they'll produce fertile offspring.

Since they are scientifically classified together, you'd think wolves and dogs would be exactly the same, but they aren't—no more than you are exactly like your sister. One rather basic difference is that dogs like to be around people and wolves don't (which must occasionally make some dog/wolf hybrids feel a little schizophrenic).

Eventually, dogs became domesticated animals instead of wild ones. No one knows why dogs accepted domestication, but they obviously found it beneficial to their survival to hook up with a human pack that would take care of them and share the bounty of the hunt in exchange for protection and guard duty. There is safety in numbers, and perhaps dogs understood that they were safer within a pack of humans rather than being hunted by humans. Or maybe dogs just liked the scent and taste of cooked meat; after all, it's difficult to roast meat over an open fire without opposable thumbs.

THE GENERIC "DOG"

All the aspects that make today's purebreds identifiable as a specific breed, such as the Papillion's big ears, the Pug's flat face, and the Great Dane's size, would go away without selective breeding (breeding to produce specific results, which is what breeders of purebred dogs and cats do). Left to their own devices to breed, dogs would select for availability above all else ("you're here, I'm here, let's make puppies, pretty mama!") and, after generations upon generations of nonselective breeding, all the *Canis familiaris* would probably look remarkably similar.

Without humans breeding for specific traits, today's dogs would eventually evolve back to what they probably were in the beginning: a medium-sized dog with a medium length brownish or brown and white coat, medium length face, and upright, prick ears. In other words, as generic a mixed breed as can be imagined. Around the world, offspring of dogs in feral populations end up looking mostly like this, whether the dogs are in South Carolina, Australia, India, Israel, Egypt, or Asia. (Northern dogs tend to have heavier coats for protection from inclement weather.)

CANINE IMMIGRANTS

As people immigrated in large numbers to America during the last couple of centuries, they brought their dogs with them. Dogs of all kinds—Belgian Sheepdogs, Pekingese, Bernese Mountain Dogs, English Toy Spaniels, West Highland White Terriers, Maltese, Norwegian Buhunds, French Bulldogs, Australian Cattle Dogs, Scottish Terriers, Rhodesian Ridgebacks, Tibetan Mastiffs, and Siberian Huskies—came to this country and mated into the Great Melting Pot. During the Great Depression and World War II, dog breeding as a hobby took a huge hit because so few people could afford to breed or to buy puppies. Dogs didn't stop mating, of course; although there were certainly still breeders operating during the 1930s and 1940s, it's likely that most matings were, shall we say, unintentional and unplanned.

Canaan dogs may look like mixed breeds, but they are an AKC-recognized breed.

During such economically difficult times as the Great Depression or immediately after immigration to a new country, many people could not afford pets. Yet some could not

afford to be without them, such as the working dogs on farms, who earned their keep. Those dogs were most likely not purebreds. Thus, the popularity of mixed breeds at the time was probably high simply because most people could not afford to breed or buy purebreds.

The American Society for Prevention of Cruelty to Animals (ASPCA) doesn't have much data on how common the practice of spaying and neutering pets was in the past and when that changed. However, regular recommendations to spay female dogs apparently began around the mid-20th century, and it was mostly related to the convenience of keeping a home clean by not having to deal with females in heat, rather than related to pet overpopulation. Even pet care books really didn't emphasize spaying and neutering until the 1960s. The ASPCA and other humane groups didn't start making spay/neuter a requirement for adoption until the early to mid-1970s, which is probably when altering pets became mainstream.

WHAT MIXED BREEDS ARE NOT

A mixed-breed dog is most easily defined by what he doesn't have: two purebred parents of the same breed. Typically, a purebred dog is thought of as one registered with a national breed club, like the American Kennel Club (AKC) in the United States or the Kennel Club (KC) in the United Kingdom, but the registration papers simply confirm a purebred heritage. A purebred dog without registration papers is still a purebred dog. If two purebred dogs of different breeds mate, such as an Irish Water Spaniel and a Boxer, then the offspring is a crossbreed of the two breeds. (Somewhat confusingly, crossbreeds are sometimes referred to as mixed-breeds as well.)

Purebred breeds are developed by taking several breeds that contain the characteristics the breeder wants and interbreeding those dogs. The breeder then keeps breeding only those dogs who have the desired characteristics. After that, only selected dogs of those with the desired characteristics are bred until the point is reached at which the animals "breed true," meaning more than 99 percent of the offspring from same breedings come out looking like their breed-standard parents. Labradoodles, for example, are not yet breeding true, and many are still crosses of Labradors and Poodles. Thus, at this time, Labradoodles are mixed breeds.

Purebreds and Predictability

What most people find appealing about purebred dogs is their inherent predictability. Golden Retrievers, for example, like to retrieve and have a nice long golden coat. Greyhounds like to run, have long faces, and short coats showing off their supermodel lack of body fat. You can usually generalize about the size, coat, exercise needs, and temperament of a purebred dog.

Advocates for purebred dogs often use the "predictability factor" to claim that purebreds make better pets than random-bred dogs. While it is a matter of opinion, "purebred" doesn't always mean "well-bred." Puppy

A mixed breed's uniqueness is one part of his most wonderful aspects.

mills and bad breeders (typically, people just in it for the money) produce registered purebred dogs that are of poor quality in terms of health and temperament; in these cases, talk of predictability goes out the window. The puppy mill Golden Retriever may still retrieve, but he may not have the Golden Retriever's hallmark sunny temperament and *joie d'vivre*.

Bad breeders cashing in on the popularity of a nice breed with good health and temperament can ruin a breed. Many fanciers of the less popular breeds often hope that their breed never hits the top 20 in AKC's list of most frequently registered breeds, because so many breeds suffer for that popularity. In the world of purebred dogs, responsible breeding is everything.

The Unique Mix

For those of us who love the no rhyme-or-reason aspects of mixed breeds, the surprise of the build or look, the amusing appearance of a dog with Basset Hound legs atop a Pug's body and a Spitz tail pluming and wagging, says it all. For people who like the unusual, purebreds pale in comparison. Really, a mixed breed's uniqueness is one of his most wonderful aspects—you'll never find another one like him. Despite being common, a mixed breed is a unique dog.

The unpredictability of the mixed breed is part of what draws their multitudinous fans to them, just as the predictability of certain traits in purebreds draw their fanciers. Many people have both purebreds and mixed-breed dogs and love them all. After all, it's always nice to have a "mix."

SO, WHAT IS HE?

A mixed-breed dog begs the question, "What do you think he is?" Guessing a mixed breed's heritage is one of those talks dog lovers love to have over and over again. It's a great conversation-starter at the dog park or obedience class. It doesn't matter what the truth is—what matters is how much fun it is discussing it. Perhaps you acquired your mix from a shelter, where the employees guessed he was part English Setter and part Belgian Sheepdog. Then you run into a breeder who guesses he's a Rat Terrier/Keeshond mix, and your vet opines he's a Shepherd/Lab mix. Large hairy dark dogs of no identifiable breed are often thought of as a Shepherd mix, whereas short-coat mixes are often labeled as a Lab mix. (Both are shelter favorites.) For all that anyone knows, he could be a German Shorthair Pointer/German Shepherd Dog/Miniature Dachshund, and the German Shorthair in question is really a mix of German Shorthair and Wirehaired Pointer. Even if you can never discover the truth, it's fun to guess.

When all you have to go on is looks, it's anyone's guess. Just because your mix is labeled an English Bulldog/Bouvier de Flanders mix doesn't mean that any Bulldog or Bouvier really *is* in there; and it doesn't mean there isn't. It's entirely possible that some genetic crap shoot of 14 other breeds ended up causing this particular dog to have a Bouvier-like face while having absolutely no genetic connection to Bouviers. At any rate, your guess as to what breed(s) are represented is just as accurate as anyone else's.

FAMOUS MIXED BREEDS

Many famous dogs in history and literature are mixed breeds: Balto, White Fang, LBJ's Yuki, Old Yeller, and all of the terrier mixes who portrayed Benji. Appropriately or not, the poster-child for mixed breeds is probably Tramp from the Disney movie *Lady and the Tramp*, in which the purebred Cocker Spaniel is a well-mannered society dog and the happy-go-lucky stray mixed breed has no discernible heritage.

Benji: The Most Famous Shelter Dog

The canine stars of the *Benji* series (both film and television) have always been mixed-breed dogs adopted at a shelter. The first "Benji" was adopted for the 1973 movie from an animal shelter in Burbank, California. Because of the publicity from that first movie, over a million dogs are thought to have been adopted from shelters.

Joe Camp, the creator of the *Benji* series, continues to emphasize pet adoption in each successive movie. In 2004's *Benji Off the Leash*, the star was found at the Humane Society of South Mississippi in Gulfport. Throughout the promotion of the movie, events were held at local shelters across the country. Joe Camp and Benji continue to provide fundraising efforts and make many appearances at shelters.

Here are a few of the more famous mixes:
- Benji from the *Benji* series of films
- Sandy from *Little Orphan Annie*
- White Fang from *White Fang,* a dog-wolf hybrid
- Buck from *The Call of the Wild*, a St. Bernard/Scotch Shepherd mix
- Winn-Dixie from *Because of Winn-Dixie*, a stray found in a grocery store
- Boy from *A Dog's Life*, a hunting breed mix
- Old Yeller from *Old Yeller*, a mixed-breed stray
- Laika, the first dog in space, a Samoyed-Husky mix
- Balto, the husky/wolf hybrid who led the last relay of the dog sled team that delivered antitoxin serum for diphtheria to Nome, Alaska, in 1925
- Tramp from *Lady and the Tramp*, the ultimate mixed breed

Mixed Breeds in the White House

The seat of power in the United States has seen its share of mixed breeds. Pushinka, a mixed-breed dog, was a gift to Caroline Kennedy from Soviet leader Nikita Khrushchev. Pushinka was the daughter of Strelka, one of the first dogs in space. The Kennedy's Welsh Terrier, Charlie, and Pushinka had a litter of pups that JFK famously called "Pupniks." Several of Caroline Kennedy's other dogs in the White House were mixed breeds: Blackie, Butterfly, and White Tip.

Lyndon Johnson's favorite dog was a mongrel, Yuki, who was found by his daughter Luci at a Texas gas station. This small stray became one of the President's favorite dogs—and Johnson had quite a few dogs (not nearly as many as Calvin Coolidge, but most presidents had less pets overall than Coolidge). Yuki got into a lot of trouble in the Oval Office: the "shocking" carpet-peeing incident in front of the Shah of Iran, and the biting of a White House police officer in the groin. Nonetheless (or perhaps because of) these events, Yuki's photo was once on the front page

Can you guess what I am? (A Saint Bernard/Great Dane mix...or a Saint Dane? I'm a Great Bernard!)

This Lab/Golden mix makes a wonderful service dog.

of the *Wall Street Journal.* Yuki often "sang" duets with Johnson while he sat on Johnson's lap, and several of those musical sessions were photographed.

Abraham Lincoln's mixed breed, Fido, described as a "brownish dog with some yellow in his coat," was not taken to the White House because the Lincolns were concerned he would not be happy or do well there. Fido was left with family friends. Before the Lincolns moved to the White House, they had a photograph taken of Fido, creating the first photograph of a presidential dog.

Mixed-Breed Heroes

Many have seen images of search-and-rescue dogs working at Ground Zero of the World Trade Center or walking through earthquake rubble. These dogs are often purebred, but many mixed breeds save lives every day. For almost half a century, a pet food manufacturer has been awarding the Dog Hero of the Year award. Over a dozen winners of the award have been mixed breeds. Many of these dogs have alerted their owners to fires, seizures, gone home to find help when a person collapsed, and performed other heroic deeds.

Actress Drew Barrymore's life was saved by her Lab/Chow mix, Flossie, whom she found as a stray. Early one morning Flossie woke up Drew and her then-husband Tom Green when their house was on fire. Barrymore, Green, and their four mixed-breed dogs escaped unharmed thanks to Flossie. After the fire, Barrymore was quoted in an interview as saying "The only thing I could think of saving was my animals, nothing else mattered. You can always buy more stuff."

Mixed-breed heroes even end up in movies. In the Clint Eastwood movie *Tightrope*, Eastwood's single father and his two daughters find a stray mixed breed in the street and bring him into

Where to Look

When looking for a dog, stay away from puppy mills. If you don't care about getting a purebred dog, look at shelters, rescues, newspapers, or search www.petfinder.org.

their household, which already has several dogs. At the end of the movie, the new stray saves the life of one of his daughters.

TO HAVE AND TO HOLD FROM THIS DAY FORWARD

However they got here, wherever they came from, mixed breeds are wildly popular. They have a kind of social chic about them. In a world that seems filled with status symbols, living with mixed breeds shows a certain level of distance or disdain for hot trends. It shows a bit of individuality and common sense to have a dog who didn't cost a fortune and has no pedigree.

Some celebrities are noted for having mixed breeds, including Jennifer Aniston, Sandra Bullock, Drew Barrymore, Orlando Bloom, Ashley Olsen, and Mischa Barton. No one who has mixed breeds when they could afford any purebred dog is looking for a canine fashion accessory. They're looking for a companion.

And what companions they are: every shape and size imaginable, and even some shapes that you can't quite imagine. Big ones, little ones, dark ones, light ones. Short stubby legs tacked on to thick wide bodies; tiny little bodies with long necks and stubby tails; long hairy coats and plumy tails or sleek, streamlined running machines with lion-like manes. Whatever we can dream up, nature can go one better.

What Does Hollywood Know About Genetics?

You've seen the movies where two different breeds mate and the female puppies look just like their mom and the boy puppies look just like their dad (*Turner & Hooch* or *Lady and the Tramp* are perfect examples). Dog lovers know this is ludicrous, but Hollywood doesn't seem to mind the fantasy. In real life, an intact purebred Cavalier King Charles Spaniel female in heat who is foolishly brought to the dog park and mated by several intact males would never have a litter that looks like all Cavaliers; apparently the producers of *Sex in the City* don't know much about dog genetics.

What Hollywood should know is that a litter of Cocker Spaniel and mixed-breed puppies would be mixed-breed puppies, maybe with big ears and a long coat; the Dogue de Bordeaux and Collie mixed puppies from *Turner & Hooch* would probably be big, with a lot of drooling from a wide jaw, and a short coat. Nature handles genetics quite well when humans aren't there.

But one thing is sure—purebred puppies don't come from the mating of two different purebreds—they would be mixed-breed puppies.

2

CHARACTERISTICS

of Mixed-Breed Dogs

Mixed breeds are seen in an awesome spectrum of sizes, coat length, weight, leg length, coloring, face length, and type of tail. You name it, it's out there. Perhaps the most adorable examples are those who appear to be piecemeal from different dogs: a Corgi's body and head with long legs and a Keeshond's plumed tail, or a Basset Hound's ears on a Whippet's lithe body. Combinations like that make people smile. Some mixed breeds look like identifiable crossbreeds, but many times the heritage of a mix is anyone's guess.

Physical traits, temperament, and the overall health of mixed breeds are a mixed bag because it all depends on unknown genetics. Puppies from two different litters parented by the same American Water Spaniel and English Setter could look like the Spaniel, the Setter, or some combination of the two. Their temperament and health issues are more of an unknown than it is for purebreds, because whatever that Golden Retriever is mixed with genetically may take precedence over the normally jolly Golden temperament. On the other hand, your Golden mix could have the wonderful temperament of a well-bred Golden.

WHAT IS HYBRID VIGOR?

Hybrid vigor is a term frequently applied to the health and longevity of mixed-breed dogs. However, people who toss it around like so much conversational salad sometimes don't quite grasp what hybrid vigor is. Detractors claim it doesn't exist, while proponents often use it to assert that any mix is automatically healthier than any purebred because of hybrid vigor. It's simply not the case.

The idea behind hybrid vigor is much like the idea of bringing Princess Diana's "commoner" genes into the Royal Family: Too much inbreeding in royal families causes problems, and you get healthier offspring if you breed outside the lines. In the dog world, crosses and mixes are thought of as healthier because they are more genetically diverse.

While there are many theories about hybrid vigor in mixed-breed dogs, none have yet been proven.

Joni Freshman, DVM, a canine reproduction specialist, says that if two healthy purebreds of different breeds mate (for example, a purebred Basset Hound and a purebred Saint Bernard), the offspring's health depends on what genes each of the purebred dogs are carrying. "While there may be no matching undesirable recessive genes, there certainly can be. Some of the genetic problems in breeds are the same, so two dogs who are themselves healthy but carry genes for the same problems (hip dysplasia, epilepsy, etc.) can produce pups with those problems."

Inbreeding Problems

Hybrid vigor suggests that dogs who are less related have, in general, increased fertility and health. "In a study done in the breeding kennels at Penn," said Dr. Freshman, "where they are breeding for lines with specific genetic disease so that they can then study those diseases, they found fertility to decrease when the coefficient of inbreeding was over about 6%. High coefficients of inbreeding have dramatically reduced fertility, lower birth weight neonates, and higher neonatal mortality. This is again related to the key point of all breeding: The more related dogs are, the less variation in the genes they carry. Some of these genes are deleterious to the dog and its ability to produce or to survive. When those are concentrated by inbreeding, more problems arise.

"If we could know for sure that the dogs we inbred had *no* deleterious genes that they were carrying, then inbreeding in and of itself would not be a problem. The issue is that we cannot at this stage of the game know this, and so the risks are there and are very real. We inbreed to fix the traits we like and want. We then risk also fixing traits we don't want."

What About Health?

You can't know if a puppy in a litter of mixed breeds will benefit from hybrid vigor. Since good health is one reason many people choose mixed breeds, it's a significant consideration, because hybrid vigor is not a given for every mixed breed—far from it. A benefit of purebred breeding is that responsible breeders (certainly not puppy mills) will have done health clearances, such as x-rays to check for hip dysplasia, to determine a given dog's health. Within one litter, health can vary, and no one can tell how healthy a puppy is just by looking.

"You can examine what is there," said Dr. Freshman. "A good physical examination should include joint manipulation, careful

Popularity

In one survey of American dog owners taken by the American Pet Products Manufacturers Association, 23 percent said they had mixed-breed dogs. While it's not possible to state that 23 percent of dogs in America are mixed breeds, this survey is one indicator of the popularity of mixed breeds.

The more related dogs are, the less variation in the genes.

What Type Is My Mix?

While no one can predict how a mixed breed will look or behave, it can be interesting to guess what type he falls into and what that means for his physical and behavioral traits. (Please note that these groupings are not official.)

Type	Example	Personality
Bully-breeds	English Bulldogs, Bull Terriers, American Staffordshire Terriers, American Pit Bull Terriers, Staffordshire Bull Terriers, Bullmastiffs, American Bulldogs	Determined, smart, can be aggressive if taught, require training
Guarding	Great Pyrenees, Dogue de Bordeaux, Kuvasz, Bouvier de Flandres, Komondor	Intelligent, dominant, brave, watchful, independent, best with experienced dog people
Herding	Collies, Australian Shepherds, Australian Cattle Dogs, Border Collies, German Shepherd Dogs, Shetland Sheepdogs, Polish Lowlands, Belgian Sheepdogs, Old English Sheepdogs	Intelligent, eager to please, loyal, affectionate, need a lot of exercise

Bull Terrier

Border Colli

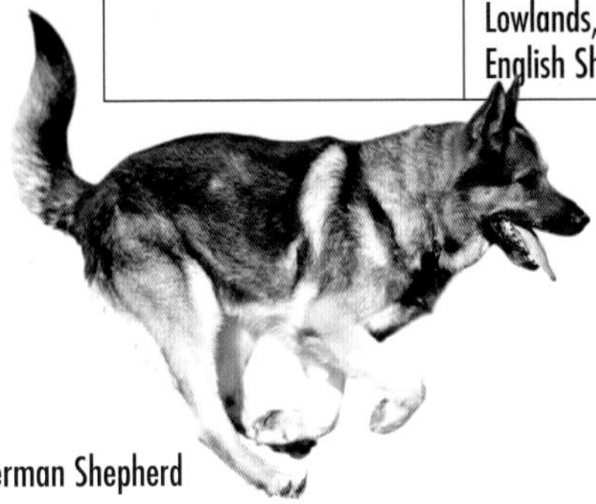

German Shepherd

Samoyed

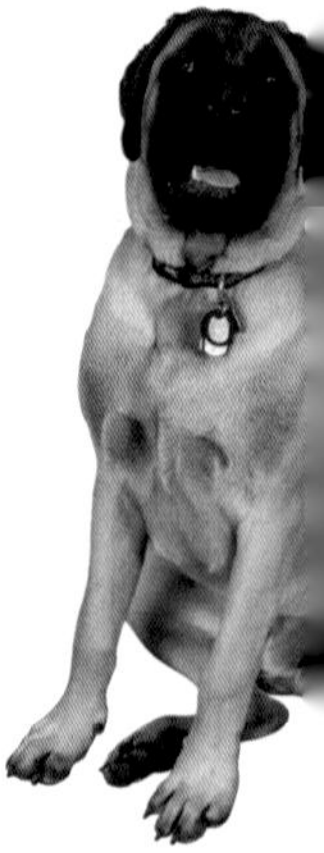

Great Pyrenees

Neapolitan Mastiff

Greyhound

English Ma

Bulldog

Type	Example	Personality
Mastiff-type	Mastiffs, Tibetan Mastiffs, Bullmastiffs, Cane Corsos, English Mastiffs, American Mastiffs, Neapolitan Mastiffs	Large, protective, need a moderate amount of exercise
Northern and Nordic	Siberian Huskies, Alaskan Malamutes, Samoyed, Finnish Spitz, Norwegian Elkhounds, Lundehunds, Swedish Vallhunds	Independent thinkers, can be difficult to train, social, affectionate, loving, need significant exercise, do not like warm climates
Sighthounds	Afghan Hounds, Whippets, Greyhounds, Pharaoh Hounds, Basenjis, Borzois, Irish Wolfhounds, Lurchers, Salukis, Scottish Deerhounds	Strong prey drive, easy to train, dignified, independent, trustworthy, need fenced-in area or will run away

ne Corso

Basenji

Whippet

ondor

American
Staffordshire Terrier

Lurcher

Siberian Husky

Afghan Hound

19

What Type Is My Mix?

Type	Example	Personality
Scenthounds	Bloodhounds, Beagles, Coonhounds, Dachshunds, Foxhounds, Harriers, Petit Basset Griffon Vendeens, Otterhounds	Stubborn, can be hard to train, amusing, intelligent, loyal, affectionate, some drool significantly
Sporting	Labrador Retrievers, Golden Retrievers, Irish Setters, Brittanys, American Water Spaniels, Cocker Spaniels, English Springer Spaniels, German Shorthaired Pointers	Need lots of exercise, rather vocal, likeable, fun, affectionate, smart, easy to train, need attention
Terriers	Cairn Terriers, Irish Terriers, Kerry Blue Terriers, Miniature Schnauzers, Scottish Terriers, Soft Coated Wheaten Terriers, West Highland White Terriers	Busy, feisty, active, need a lot of exercise, strong prey drive, smart, affectionate, vocal

Dachshund

Beagle

Scottish Terrier

Labrador Retriever

German Shorthaired Pointer

Pug

Golden Retriever

Great D

Type	Example	Personality
Toys	Toy Poodles, Cavalier King Charles Spaniels, Chihuahuas, Havanese, Maltese, Papillons, Pekingese, Pomeranians, Pugs, Shih Tzu, Yorkshire Terriers	Lap companions, smart, stubborn, loyal, can be difficult to housetrain, excellent apartment pets, affectionate, people-oriented
Working	Boxers, Doberman Pinschers, Great Danes, Akitas, Giant and Standard Schnauzers, Newfoundlands, Rottweilers, Saint Bernards	Intelligent, easy to train, need significant exercise, need a "job" to keep them occupied, loyal, best for experienced owners

Chihuahua

Rottweiler

Yorkshire Terrier

Doberman Pinscher

Miniature Schnauzer

Cocker Spaniel

Maltese

Newfoundland

Pariahs

Some mixed breeds resemble the quintessential pariah dog, which are feral or wild dog populations living near human settlements; how closely they look like a pariah dog depends on how far away they are from purebred lines.

examination of the mouth and teeth, fundic examination of the retina, and good auscultation of the chest for murmurs. If the potential owner wishes to do so, and the mixed breed is one at risk for liver problems, blood work could be performed to look for a clue. PennHip evaluation for hip dysplasia can be performed on dogs as young as 4 months of age, but that does require anesthesia. This is one area where it can help to buy a purebred from a reliable breeder. For instance, I can tell potential puppy buyers what has and has not shown up in several generations of my dogs, including all the siblings. When you choose a mixed-breed puppy, you typically have no family medical history to evaluate."

PHYSICAL TRAITS

As we discussed in Chapter 1, appearances can be deceiving. If you are unsure of your mix's parentage, you'll have to make a reasonable guess based on appearance. Sometimes the answers about heritage are relatively (pun intended) straightforward. Dr. Joni Freshman, DVM, thinks people who are familiar with a variety of breeds, such as veterinarians, are fairly good at determining which breeds are in a mix, unless there is too much mixture (i.e., several generations of varied mixes). "There are clear characteristics that define most breeds, and their presence is a big clue," said Dr. Freshman. "I frequently am called upon to do rescue for the varieties of Belgian Shepherd Dog. Quite frequently, the dogs I am called to the shelter to identify are not Belgian Tervuren, but Chow and German Shepherd Dog mixes. They have *none* of the defining characteristics of the Belgian, but several from the Chow and German Shepherd."

The following physical and behavioral descriptions are nothing more than guesses. No one can predict exactly how a given mixed breed will look or behave, but you can have a general idea. If your mixed breed is a mix of two working breeds, you will likely have a large, strong, smart dog who needs a job, although appearance depends heavily on genetics. If you have a mix from two of the American Kennel Club groups (herding, toy, working, terrier, etc.) no one can predict with any accuracy what you'll end up with. However, the guessing game of heritage is always a fun conversation topic.

Your vet, trainer, or shelter workers can all help you guess your mix's background. Here are some very broad general traits for different groups of dogs that might make up your mix's heritage.

Bully-Breeds

Bully-breeds tend to have short coats that are easy to groom. Their bodies are heavier in weight than you'd think from looking at them, and they are generally medium to large dogs (mostly large). Colors range from white, brindle, brown, fawn, and so on; some have markings while some have solid coats. Some have short flat (brachycephalic) faces that make breathing difficult, such as Bulldogs, but others like Bull Terriers don't, so their breathing ability and tolerance of heat depends on their facial structure. Many have prick ears. Some breeds in this category include English Bulldogs, Bull Terriers, American Staffordshire Terriers, American Pit Bull Terriers, Staffordshire Bull Terriers, Bullmastiffs, and American Bulldogs.

Guarding

Guarding dogs are generally large, powerful, muscular dogs. Independent thinkers, they can manage a flock without human direction. Colors are all over the map, from solid long white coats to short fawn coats. Examples breeds include Great Pyrenees, Dogue de Bordeaux, Mastiffs, Kuvasz, Bouvier de Flandres, and Alaskan Malamutes.

Based on looks, it appears this mix has some Beagle in him.

Herding

Most herders have long hair and long ears, and come in a variety of colors. They can have short legs like Corgis (designed to get out of the way quickly while working with cattle) or long ones like Belgian Tervuren, who guard sheep. Size ranges from medium to giant. Colors range from grays and browns generally mixed with white. Breeds include Collies, Australian Shepherds, Australian Cattle Dogs, Border Collies, German Shepherd Dogs, Shetland Sheepdogs, Polish Lowlands, Belgian Sheepdogs, and Old English Sheepdogs.

Mastiff-type

Mastiffs are heavy-framed large- to giant-sized dogs who require experienced owners. They are ancient breeds, and are often used for working, carting, and guarding. They need a moderate amount of exercise. Breeds include Mastiffs, Tibetan Mastiffs, Dogue de Bordeaux, Bullmastiffs, Cane Corsos, English Mastiffs, and American Mastiffs.

You can see some of the physical traits of the Bouvier des Flandres breed in this mix.

Northern and Nordic

These small to large dogs are bred for winter climates. Northern breeds are sometimes called *spitzes,* and are stocky, heavy-coated breeds. They sometimes look like wolves, and usually have prick ears. Nordic dogs are called such because of their countries of origin, such as Norway, Sweden, and Finland. They generally have thick double coats to keep them warm, so they shed a lot of long hair. Their ears are quite thick. Northern breeds include Siberian Huskies, Alaskan Malamutes, and Samoyed. Nordic breeds include Finnish Spitz, Norwegian Elkhounds, Lundehunds, and Swedish Vallhunds.

Sighthounds

Sighthounds are dogs who hunt on instinct when they see prey moving and overtake that prey using their speed. Size

This mix loves working in the water.

ranges from toy to giant. Colors are often shades of brown and tan but also white mixed with other colors (particolor). Breeds include Whippets, Italian Greyhounds, Pharaoh Hounds, Basenjis, Borzois, Irish Wolfhounds, Lurchers, Salukis, and Scottish Deerhounds.

Scenthounds

These dogs hunt by smell, not sight. Most of these breeds have long drooping ears like Basset Hounds, large nasal cavities, loose wet lips that often drool, and booming voices that can almost wake the dead. They don't have to be fast because they don't keep their prey in sight, but rather follow the scent. They can follow a scent over ground and water even when the scent is several days old. Size ranges from medium to large. Colors are usually brown earth tones. Breeds include Bloodhounds, Beagles, Coonhounds, Dachshunds, Foxhounds, Harriers, Petit Basset Griffon Vendeens, and Otterhounds.

Sporting

Sporting dogs are large dogs who make great companions—as long as you like lots of exercise. Spaniels flush birds up into the air, retrievers carry back dead birds and ducks, pointers and setters first "set" (a kind of physical motion like a sit, but not exactly) and then point at game. Most have drop ears. They have a wide range of colors from golden to tan to black to white. Breeds include Labrador Retrievers, Irish Setters, Brittanys, American Water

Play Ball!

Different mixes have different personalities. Here's how a retriever mix, terrier mix, and senior mixed-breed dog might view a game of ball.

Retriever-mix Austin: There's a ball!

Terrier-mix Ginger: That big dog always gets there first.

Senior-mix Fred: dum de dum

Retriever-mix Austin: It's in the air! It's in my mouth!

Terrier-mix Ginger: I want that ball too. Fork it over!

Senior-mix Fred: Hey, a ball! Oh, here's a bug. Cool.

Retriever-mix Austin: yay yay yay for balls! Tennis balls rock!

Terrier-mix Ginger: Hey, stop that!!! She threw that ball for me!!!

Senior-mix Fred: Huh? Where did mom throw what ball? Look, grass.

Retriever-mix Austin: Slimy airborne balls are the best! Yay yay yay!

Terrier-mix Ginger: You don't need two balls. *Mom!* Austin's got my ball again!

Senior-mix Fred: Oh look, Ginger's poop. No, it's Austin's. No, it's Ginger's.

Retriever-mix Austin: There's a ball! In the air! Mine! Mine! Mine!

Terrier-mix Ginger: Fine. I'll just chew this stick to shreds.

Senior-mix Fred: Why did a ball just land next to my head?

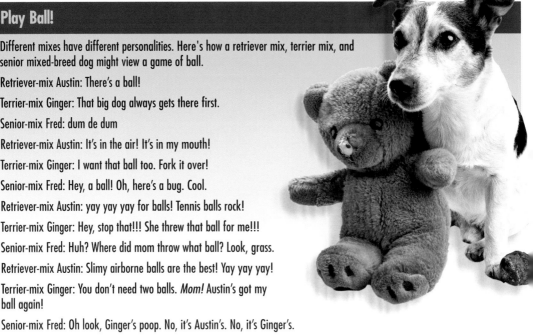

Spaniels, Cocker Spaniels, English Springer Spaniels, and German Shorthaired Pointers.

Terriers

Terriers generally are small or medium-sized dogs (exceptions include Airdales and Staffordshire Terriers). Prick or dropped ears are generally the norm, and they often keep their tails rather than having them docked, as many sporting dogs do. Colors are seen in a full range of solid white, blues (a type of gray), browns, and brindles. Some terriers dislike other animals, including dogs. Many terriers have wiry coats, but some have soft nonshedding coats. Breeds include Cairn Terriers, Irish Terriers, Kerry Blue Terriers, Miniature Schnauzers, Scottish Terriers, Soft Coated Wheaten Terriers, and West Highland White Terriers.

Toys

A toy dog is defined as being under 20 pounds (9.0 kg), although most of us think of toys as dogs under 10 pounds (4.5 kg). Some breeds are bred down from larger sizes and look like miniatures of the larger breed, such as an Italian Greyhound. Many require professional grooming, and most have hair that does not shed. Breeds include Toy Poodles, Cavalier King Charles Spaniels, Chihuahuas, Havanese, Maltese, Papillons, Pekingese, Pomeranians, Pugs, Shih Tzu, and Yorkshire Terriers.

Working

Working dogs guard property, pull sleds, perform military tasks, and save lives with their search-and-rescue abilities (trained or otherwise). They are usually large, strong dogs. Because of their size and strength, they need owners who can train them correctly, but training is easy because of their native intelligence. Colors range from the solid white of the Kuvasc to the solid black of the Newfoundland. Breeds include Boxers, Doberman Pinschers, Great Danes, Akitas, Giant and Standard Schnauzers, Rottweilers, and Saint Bernards.

This Lab mix still has retrieving in his blood.

BEHAVIORAL TRAITS

Mixed-breed dogs are lovable, intelligent, sweet, wonderful, and have a wild array of characteristics. Some mixed breeds exhibit distinct behavioral traits derived from certain groups of dogs, whereas others don't. If your mix happens to be a mix of breeds from the same group, the dog will probably have the group's traits in abundance. For example, if the dog is a Border Collie/Australian Shepherd mix, you could see a small puppy herding your kids and playing endlessly at high speed with balls. A Norwich Terrier/Kerry Blue Terrier mix would likely be feisty, energetic, barky, and probably dig holes while hunting vermin under the deck or in the middle of your yard. An English Setter/English Springer Spaniel would demand tea (kidding!) and have tons of energy, possibly more than you would really enjoy, chase birds, and be a sweetie pie.

The behavior commonality probably applies more to crossbreeds, which are the offspring of two different purebred dogs. Once the mix includes more than two breeds, the less predictable those traits are going to be.

Here are some very general guidelines to what type of personality or behavior you might expect from certain groups. Of course, every dog is an individual, and your mix is no exception!

Bully-breeds

Bully-breeds can be intimidating, and these are the dogs most feared by the general public. They can be aggressive, but aren't naturally so unless their owner has encouraged them to be aggressive. They are determined, smart, and seek approval from their owner. They require training and do well at it.

Herding

Herding is a type of modified predatory behavior. Typically, herding dogs nip at the heels of the animals they're herding. In terms of being a family dog, they can get a bit distraught when their herd is not kept together, and will do their best to keep you together when walking as a group. If parents aren't around, herders sometimes step up and herd or nip small children. They are wonderfully intelligent, eager to please, loyal, and affectionate, and they make great pets as long as they get enough exercise.

Guarding

Guarding dogs are intelligent, dominant, and independent thinkers. They will confront any perceived enemy or intruder, so early obedience training is a must. They must be independent thinkers to guard a flock or property, although guarding instincts range from polite minimal resistance to outright hostility; no one will steal your television without notice. Generally speaking, it takes an experienced person to own guard dogs because, in the wrong hands, they will become too dominant. Most are calm in the house, and they are brave, watchful, independent, and resourceful.

Mastiff-Type

These are ancient breeds and are often used for working, carting, and guarding. They need a moderate amount of exercise. Because of their size, they absolutely must have obedience training at a young age, but they do not need protection training because that is instinctive. Many make excellent family pets.

Northern and Nordic

These dogs are bred for winter climates, and are not all that fond of hot southern summers. They are ecstatic romping through snow—whether it's pulling sleds or just playing. They are independent thinkers and sometimes difficult to train, yet they are very social. Most are friendly toward people and affectionate. Although they don't make good guard dogs, some can be aggressive toward other animals. They need significant exercise, but are prized as companions.

Sighthounds

Sighthounds can run far faster than you ever could; the Greyhound is the fastest sighthound and has been clocked at 40 mph. They must be fenced for their own safety because they

Toy mixes can be "lap angels."

will otherwise take off at the sight of something that looks like prey. Small pocket pets like mice or rats are not usually safe around them. They make great family pets, and train nicely.

Scenthounds

These dogs are pretty stubborn, and can be hard to train because of that stubbornness, but they can be quite amusing. Intelligent, they make loyal family pets as long as you're not looking for snap-to obedience. Some drool significantly. Because they were historically bred to hunt together, dogs were selected partially on the basis of non-aggressiveness.

Sporting

Sporting dogs make great companions as long as you like lots of exercise. They are noted for being rather vocal. Likeable and fun to be around, they make wonderful family dogs, and are affectionate and smart.

Terriers

Busy, feisty, and active, many terriers are the canine version of hyperactive children, so they need a lot of exercise. They make excellent watch dogs. Energetic dogs with a real zest for enjoying life, they usually want to be part of everything going on around them. Some—but not all—are fairly aggressive toward other dogs. Some terriers dislike other animals, and most small pocket pets (like rats) are not safe around them. They are smart, affectionate, and they make great—albeit vocal—family dogs.

Toys

Delightful companions fit for a lap, many are smart, stubborn, and rule the roost. Some are notoriously difficult to housetrain. They make great watch dogs because their barking alerts you to intruders. They can usually get sufficient exercise indoors and therefore make excellent pets for apartment dwellers or senior citizens. They are affectionate and great lap warmers. They are usually people-oriented and like regular human companionship.

Working

Working dogs were bred to work, so most of them are unhappy without a job of their own. They do not want to spend their lives on the couch. These intelligent dogs train quickly. They need significant exercise. Because of their size and intelligence, they are not necessarily good family dogs, even though they are very loyal. They generally require experienced owners and a lot of obedience training.

Sadly, some mixed breeds can inherit only the worst aspects of each parent's personality. Some poodle mixes can be really high strung, and many "designer dog" blends involve poodles (see section below on Designer Dogs). Some small-dog mixes can be neurotic and destructive. Guard-dog mixes can be frighteningly dominant-aggressive and difficult to train because of their dominant nature; these dogs require highly experienced, confident dog owners. That's why temperament testing, which is discussed in Chapter 3, is critical.

Can you guess what I am? (A Schnauzer/Poodle cross. I'm a Schnoodle!)

THE FUSS ABOUT DESIGNER DOGS

The concept of designer dogs is controversial. The term *designer dog* refers to crossbreed combinations that have been bred on purpose rather than randomly.

Examples of designer dogs include:

- Bulloxer: American Bull Dog/Boxer
- Cavachon: Bichon Frise/Cavalier King Charles Spaniel
- Cockapoo: Cocker Spaniel/Poodle
- Goldendoodle: Golden Retriever/Poodle
- Labradoodle: Labrador Retriever/Poodle
- Maltipoo: Maltese/Poodle
- Pekepoo: Pekingese/Poodle
- Pomapoo: Pomeranian/Poodle
- Poochin: Poodle/Japanese Chin
- Puggle: Pug/Beagle
- Schnoodle: Miniature Schnauzer/Poodle
- Schnu: Miniature Schnauzer/Shiba Inu
- Westshire Terrier: West Highland Terrier/Yorkshire Terrier
- Whoodles: Soft Coated Wheaten/Poodle

Many "designer dogs," like this Peke-a-Poo, use Poodles because of their desirable hair type.

Many of these dogs are touted as low shedders (there is no such thing as a completely non-shedding dog, just ones that shed significantly less than others), so that people with allergies have a better chance of finding a dog they can tolerate. The vast majority of these crosses use Poodles, most likely because of the Poodle's low shedding and above-average intelligence.

Breeders producing designer dogs claim that crossbreeds are healthier than purebreds because of first-generation hybrid vigor. They then sell the puppies for a lot of money, sometimes more than you would pay for a purebred dog. As we discussed earlier, hybrid vigor is not a sure thing in any mixed breed. Any breeder worth her salt must do health tests on her breeding stock.

Designer-dog breeders often claim they can have some level of predictability about a mixed-breed dog by looking at the temperaments of the parents. That may be so when both parents are purebred, but not if there has been a lot of crossing back and forth.

No designer dog is currently recognized by the American Kennel Club (AKC), United Kennel Club (UKC), or the Kennel Club (KC). According to the AKC, a breed requires at least three generations of dogs with highly consistent offspring from hundreds of litters to certify as a new breed, and at this time no designer dog fits that description. Fanciers of both Cockapoos and Labradoodles have created national dog clubs, but at the moment, designer dogs are expensive mixed breeds.

Cockapoos are thought of as the "original designer dog."

Hypo-Allergenic Dogs?

The biggest concern with some designer dogs, Labradoodles in particular, is that they are marketed as non-shedding (because of their Poodle half). Yet many of them shed like Labs! Most designer dogs are first-generation (i.e., a Labrador Retriever bred to a Standard Poodle to create a Labradoodle), and their characteristics cannot be predicted. There is no reason to assume that each puppy from each first-generation litter will get the Poodle's non-shedding coat. (Anecdotally, if the mother is the Lab, the puppies may shed more than Labradoodles whose mother was a Poodle.) Many people who are looking for a hypo-allergenic big dog end up with a dog who sheds like a Lab.

"Labrador retrievers are the breed about which I have received the most shedding complaints in my 21 years of practice as a veterinarian," said Dr. Freshman. "While poodles don't shed, there is no guarantee that a particular pup or grandpup won't do so."

Designer Dogs Profiles

The original "poo" mix, well known far before the designer dog era, is the cockapoo. One could say that they began the designer dog trend of making mixed breeds so incredibly fashionable. But of all the designer dogs to date, Labradoodles seem to be at the forefront of the trend, and will undoubtedly remain wildly popular for years to come.

Cockapoos

Cockapoos, the original designer dog, are crosses of purebred Cocker Spaniels and Poodles. They are adorable little fluff balls that range up to about 19 pounds (8.5 kg). The cross has been popular since the 1960s, and fanciers have created the Cockapoo Club of America, although they have no intention of trying to join the AKC. Their web site states, "This type of cross breeding results in 'hybrid vigor' in which the best qualities of each breed manifest in the offspring. This, however, assumes that one is not breeding from defective/impure Cockers or Poodles."

The Club has a code of ethics, and has created a rating system for breeders. They require that breeders of Cockapoos take back any dog within his lifetime, which is what all responsible breeders do, as well as screen buyers carefully. The Club's overall goal is "to breed down the generations of unrelated AKC-provable Cockapoos to establish the Cockapoo as a breed keeping good ethics, health and temperament first and foremost."

As of now, Labradoodles are not "breeding true," as you can see from these examples of the dogs.

What's particularly nice about the Cockapoo Club is the effort extended to create healthy dogs with nice temperaments. Members of the Club who breed their dogs are expected to provide copies to the Club of the parent's AKC papers, as well as the Canine Eye Registry Foundation (CERF) certificate, Orthopedic Foundation for Animals (OFA) patellar luxation, elbow, and hip certificates. Proof that the breeders are starting to develop beyond the first generation is to be given to the Club, which is developing a registry. They also have a Cockapoo rescue.

Labradoodles

Brought into vogue in the late 1980s, these hybrids have become very popular. Labradoodles were first conceived in Australia for use as guide or service dogs who don't shed. Standard Poodles, who have a desirable type of coat, tend to be a bit too smart and independent for service dog work, but when mixed with the eager-to-please Labrador, they have the makings of terrific service dogs.

Several owners have wanted Labradoodles because of the alleged non-shedding factor, and have been mightily disappointed by the excessive level of shedding. Some first-generation Labradoodles don't shed, and some shed slightly less than Labs. It's a genetic crap shoot. As a matter of fact, the practice of breeding them for service dogs was discontinued in Australia because too many of them shed.

Dog Park Rule

Always pick up your dog's poop and dispose of it in the designated container.

Because of the number of first-generation offspring, a lot of Labradoodles don't resemble each other very much. They're all incredibly cute—they just aren't necessarily cute in exactly the same way.

Some dog trainers notice that many of the Labradoodles in obedience class are rather hyper and have a tough time settling down, and some who are a little too sensitive may have problems with submissive urination (although this can happen in any breed).

WHAT KIND OF PET WILL HE BE?

Because of the nature of mixed breeds, there is no single answer to the question of what kind of pet one particular mixed breed will be. It depends on your idea of what makes a good pet and how well you can determine the temperament and type of dog you're considering.

City or Country?

Some dogs are better suited to apartment living than others, but it's not all related to size. On the contrary, some tiny dogs deemed fit for apartment life are hyper and noisy, whereas some gentle giants are quiet and calm inside and out. A dog's suitability to apartment life depends more on temperament than size, as long as the dog isn't so big that there isn't room to move around the furniture.

Grooming Requirements

Grooming doesn't just make your dog look good, it contributes to good health. Hair mats can pull on the skin, getting hair out of eyes can help prevent eye infections, trimming nails makes walking and getting exercise more comfortable and enjoyable. Since it must be done for the dog's well-being, be sure to figure out before you get the dog how much time you will regularly have available for grooming and if you're willing to pay and go to appointments with a professional groomer. Regular brushing is needed with most mixed breeds, unless yours is a very short-haired mix like a Boxer/Greyhound.

Exercise: A Tired Dog Is a Good Dog

Every dog, excluding times of illness, needs lifelong exercise. How much exercise depends on the dog. With the hallmark predictability of purebreds, you know that a Border Collie has to have major exercise, and as a highly intelligent breed, will find incredibly creative ways to get that exercise—and you are pretty much guaranteed not to like all of the results. Any Border Collie mix will need a ton of exercise, and there's no room for excuses such as bad weather.

Any mix that involves a herding or hunting background will need significant exercise all his life. Mixes that involve nonsporting backgrounds will have varying levels of need for exercise; Dalmatian mixes will need more than a Bichon Frise mix or Bulldog mix. Working dogs will need more exercise than toy mixes. (Regardless of parentage, puppies and younger dogs need more exercise than senior dogs.)

Exercise does not have to consist of full out running and playing in a large space, but that certainly helps tone down the energy level. Long leashed walks are fine and, as a plus, you get to know the neighbors and their dogs.

Dog Park Rule #2

Never bring a female in heat to a dog park.

Dog Parks

Dog parks, when used appropriately, can be terrific places. Dogs and dog people can socialize, walk, exercise, communicate, and be outside together. Dogs can find other dogs who enjoy their level of exercise: distance ball chasing or just following behind a person's heels. The dog park is a social event for both dogs and people, and you get to know other dog people who feel the same way about dogs as you do. Some dogs are happier at the dog park than anywhere else. (I know mine are.)

Some dog parks are fenced and some aren't, but even within a fenced park your dog should be under voice control. Some parks have areas designated for puppies and small dogs only.

Pet-supply stores offer a variety of toys designed for outdoor exercise that you can use at the dog park, such as the plastic ball thrower that tosses a ball farther than if you throw it, flying discs in many shapes (even squirrel shaped), neoprene toys for use in the water, regular balls, and balls that bounce erratically. Indoor toys like squeaky toys should remain at home.

If your dog is dog aggressive or dog reactive, don't bring him to the dog park—someone is bound to get hurt. If your dog can't play nice with others, find another avenue for exercise. Dog parks can be the best place on the planet until problem dogs arrive—the ones who should be wearing T-shirts stating "doesn't play well with others"—and then the situation deteriorates in moments.

Dog parks can be terrific places to take your mixed breed.

If your dog gets into a fight, *whether he started it or not*, it's your responsibility to break it up. Letting the dogs "work it out between themselves" can lead to expensive veterinary bills, ruined temperaments, and fatalities. A loud noise like an air horn or pouring cold water over the fight can help break things up; standing off to the side and saying "No, Sly, stop that! SLY!" does not help—it's the equivalent of a raindrop in a drought. Pull a dog's tail to drag him out of it; don't put your hand in the middle of the action. You can be bitten pulling on a collar to get your dog away.

Children and Dogs

Like peas and carrots, kids and dogs belong together. Because many families with young children are by necessity careful with finances, many people grow up with a mixed breed. Even though their parents could not afford a purebred, most people wouldn't trade that wonderful mixed breed they grew up with for anything in the world.

While dogs and kids are a natural pairing, small children and dogs need supervision when together, and they need to learn the guidelines you have established. Children must be taught at a young age how to act appropriately around dogs. Puppies in particular need to be protected from children who are screaming and playing wildly, because they can unintentionally hurt the puppy, causing a fearful attitude toward children that may last for a lifetime. Have your children follow basic guidelines:

Falling for the Underdog

In a shelter or rescue situation, it's hard not to feel sorry for a dog that's obviously having a hard time. The frightened, terrified dog who just needs love usually has a heartbreaking background—dumped in an alley, turned into the shelter because his owner died, thrown out a car window. It's too much for a real dog person to fathom. That dog *needs* me, you think.

Think again. While all of that is true, it's also true that there are more good dogs available than there are good homes. It's a sad fact that breaks many dog lovers' hearts. But it doesn't mean that you should spend the next 10 to 15 years with a fearful, aggressive dog who is angry at the world, no matter how soft and kind your heart is.

It's a mistake I once made. I adopted a 6-month-old Basenji/Husky mix who was so cowed by being in the shelter that she couldn't even walk. She shook with terror the entire time we were in the meeting room, but she eventually took a huge leap of faith and gingerly stepped into my lap. It was the bravest thing I've ever seen.

That was the only time in 15 years that she sat on my lap. She didn't do well at the dog park, she didn't do well at obedience class, she didn't do well at my sister's house, she generally didn't do well in life. Berkeley was a hard dog to love because of her fear of the world. She had a string of unfortunate but appropriate nicknames: Satan's Child, Beloved Demon Spawn, The Berkinator, Devil Dog, and my personal favorite (and the most sarcastic), Miss Congeniality. Her daily wolverine impersonations meant I spent a lot of time with my hand over her snarled snout. She was, as they say, in touch with her anger.

Did I love her? Yes, with all my heart. I miss her still. But will I get another dog like her? Not if you paid me. She was trouble almost every day, and she made it to 15 years of age (my father insisted that only the good die young). She bit people. She snapped at children. She escaped frequently—a real Houdini hound. Her wolverine impersonation was intimidating. She disliked most other dogs. Sadly, I didn't know enough about dogs then to help her, and I've felt guilty about her for years. Many people told me that nobody else would have kept her, but I know that isn't true. I do believe there are some other people who would have done a better job with her.

So, before you choose some poor underdog who has problems with the world at large, remind yourself that life with a happy, cheerful dog who doesn't have emotional problems means you will have less problems and liability.

- No hitting
- No screaming
- No pulling fur
- No table feeding
- Leave the dog alone when he wants to be left alone

Any mixed-breed dog, from the tiny toy mixes to the hulking 150 pounders (68 kg), should be treated with respect by children. The smaller mixed breeds tend to dislike shrieking and the general noise level from toddlers; toddlers must be supervised around all dogs at all times. Some fearful dogs are nervous around the quick movements of young children. However, children who are taught to be respectful will be safer around dogs and will grow up thinking about treating others with respect.

Your children will learn to be responsible around dogs by following your lead. Children can also learn responsibility by taking care of age-appropriate tasks. Even very young children can help out by carrying a food can, choosing a new toy, or bringing the empty food bowl to you for washing. Older children can help walk the dog, bathe the dog, go to the veterinarian's, and so on. As children age, give them increasing levels of responsibility for the dog.

Teach your child how to interact appropriately with dogs.

PREPARING
for Your Mixed-Breed Dog

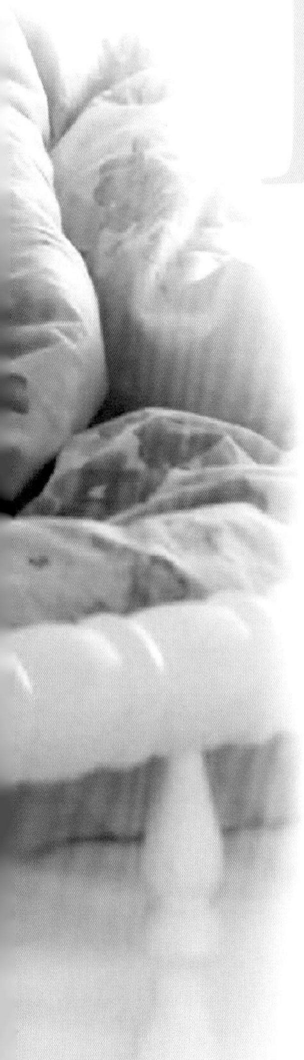

ecause mixed-breed dogs are so cute and are often free or inexpensive, people sometimes get them on impulse, without thinking through whether or not they really want a dog. You find one abandoned on the side of the road and you take him home, thinking you'll find a good home for him—and you do, at your house. As often happens with kind-hearted souls, the stray becomes a member of the family.

Many people spend more time planning a vacation than they spend thinking about adding another pet to the family. Ask yourself some honest questions:

- Can you afford a pet? The cost of vet bills and food over a dog's lifetime are not insignificant considerations, and then there are obedience classes, toys, licenses, and equipment like crates, bowls, leashes, and collars.
- Is your living situation such that a landlord, roommate, or spouse will not insist that there is no room for a dog?
- If you already have a few dogs, are you zoned for more?
- Are you doing it for the kids? Even if your child promises to take care of the dog, understand that the bottom line is that an adult usually ends up being the main caretaker.

Should you decide, after prudent examination and considering your existing animal population, that you have enough room in your home, heart, schedule, and wallet for a dog, then you are ready to go. Except for the purchase price, there's no difference in deciding to bring home a mixed breed or purebred; either you have the ability and desire to have a dog, or you don't.

Lack of time to take care of a dog is one reason dogs end up in shelters or rescue. American society is busy, a bit like a large ant colony in constant motion. Many people find they don't have the time for everything they want to do. Dogs are social creatures who need human companionship, and they cannot be alone all during the business day and alone again in the evening. If you think you have time for a dog but aren't sure, try fostering a dog for the local shelter or rescue so that you only have a short-term commitment.

PUPPY VERSUS ADULT

Happiness may be a warm puppy, but there are some valid reasons to get an adult instead of a puppy. The up side of puppies is that they are incredibly cute and full of life. Puppies elicit human responses that seem independent of our will. You can't help but turn into mush. When your new puppy snuggles up in your arms and falls asleep, and he settles in with a deep sigh as you kiss the top of his head, all is right with the world. Another plus is that you can train puppies the way you want without having to undo someone else's mistakes or lack of effort. You will have known each other for the dog's entire life.

The down side is that puppies require far more work than adult dogs do; between the housetraining, obedience training, exercise to burn off that massive puppy energy, cleaning up trash and buying replacement shoes because he chewed them up, you have a lot of work before you.

You can find puppies at shelters, but keep in mind that puppies can be a lot of work!

If you haven't had a puppy in a long time, you tend to forget how much work they are, particularly if you've been living with a canine senior citizen whose exercise needs are fulfilled by going around the block on sunny days. More than anything else, the main concern with puppies is providing sufficient exercise so that you'll have a dog who is relatively calm by the end of the day.

Adopting an adult dog has many benefits. He'll usually arrive already housetrained or just in need of a refresher course, he's probably had had some basic training, and he's not teething (chewing everything in sight). You know exactly what the dog is going to look like when he's grown up, because he is grown up. But the best advantage is that you have seen the dog's temperament and know what you're dealing with.

Some people think that only puppies bond with new owners, but that couldn't be further from the truth. Adult dogs bond to their new owners even more strongly than a dog who hasn't known anyone else; rehomed dogs know that it's possible to lose a home, and they hold on tight to their new family. The depth and passion of bonding with an adult dog is often stronger than with a puppy.

A wonderful adult may be waiting for you at a shelter.

Some of that bonding is separation anxiety, and it's common enough to be the down side of adopting an adult. Another down side to adult adoption is that you don't know exactly what his past holds and how that will affect behavior. If your adult rescue has issues with brooms, it's a pretty easy guess as to why: Someone smacked the dog with a broom. But that's an easy cause-and-effect situation. Some dogs have such difficult pasts that you may need the services of an experienced and compassionate trainer or behaviorist before your adopted dog is who you envisioned.

WHERE TO FIND THE DOG OF YOUR DREAMS

There are many places to find the mixed breed of your dreams—shelters, rescues, pet stores, breeders, even newspaper ads. Regardless where you get your mix, you'll need to look out for some important issues. Make sure the dog looks healthy. Are his eyes clear and shiny? What condition is his coat? Does he have any nasal discharge? Find out if your formal adoption or purchase is accompanied by a health guarantee, (i.e., if you take the dog to the vet and immediately discover a health issue you do not want to

Puppy Costs

If you get a puppy, remember that the first year is typically the most expensive.

take care of, you want to have the option of returning the dog and getting your money back). Even if you wouldn't return the dog no matter what, it's best to have the option. The ability to return the dog also says much about the group's ethics and true concern for animals.

Shelter

Mixed breeds can always be easily found at any shelter. Shelters are full of nice mixed breeds who are there through no fault of their own; shelters are also full of dogs who are there because their previous owners did not bother to train them, then decided they couldn't live with dogs who jump up on visitors or beg at the table. Generally, dogs end up at shelters for reasons more related to the previous owner than to the dog himself. Those reasons have nothing to do with whether the dog will make a good pet, but typically have everything to do with whether or a not a person is a responsible dog owner. Dogs end up in a shelter because:

- The prior owner had no time.
- He needs too much exercise.
- He is out of control (often a sign of no training).
- Someone in the family is allergic.
- The prior owner doesn't want the responsibility.

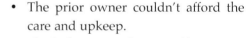

Mixed breeds can be found at any shelter.

- The prior owner couldn't afford the care and upkeep.
- The kids won't take care of him.
- He's chewing (often a sign of no training or too little exercise).

Puppies aren't born trained; that's their owner's responsibility, and some people don't care to put in enough time to train their dogs. If you don't have time for training, start out with an adult dog who has already had basic training.

Occasionally, dogs are given up because they are aggressive or ill. No matter what the story was from the people giving up the dog, the shelter employees will soon figure out if either of these are true. Severely aggressive dogs won't be adopted out; however, illnesses may be easier to manage or cure than the previous owners realized.

Shelters provide a wonderful place for people to find dogs who deserve a second chance and a good home.

When You Go to the Shelter

When you go to a shelter, you will be asked questions about your background and living conditions. Shelters usually check out personal and veterinary references as well as owning/renting conditions before allowing the dog to go to a new home; these rules are to prevent a quick return of dogs who are already stressed. Believe it or not, some people try to sneak dogs into rented properties that don't allow pets, and then landlords insist that the dog be removed. To avoid that scenario, shelters usually check on that information before adopting a dog out.

At the shelter, you can meet and interact with the dog you are interested in.

If you see a dog you like at the shelter, before you meet and greet with that dog on a one-on-one basis, Chelse Wieland, a canine behavior consultant, recommends talking to an employee who has information about that dog. Once you get your hands on a dog, your heart takes over instead of your head, so ask questions before you ask to take the dog out for a get-together. If there aren't any red flags, then ask to meet the dog in person. Then you can fall in love.

Every shelter should have some record of the dog's behavior, whether it's just notes on the door like "didn't like people coming into the kennel" or "gave back ball when asked during walk." Volunteers' written notes are helpful.

Wieland, who used to work in a shelter, suggests that you look for facilities that have help for adopters when problems come up; don't hesitate to contact the shelter if you're worried about something. That way, you can stay on top of the issue, and with

The shelter or rescue will match you with a mix that is right for your family.

Obedience Classes

A correlation exists between a dog's behavior and being given up for adoption. Don't pass on basic obedience because of the cost of the classes.

proper help. some things can be turned around.

Rescue

Rescue groups are formed by fanciers of certain breeds to help find unwanted dogs permanent homes. Some purebred rescue groups occasionally take in a mixed-breed dog who appears to be mostly the breed in question (i.e., English Setter Rescue takes in a mixed breed who has enough of an English Setter's characteristics to be a dog mixed with English Setter). Unlike shelters, rescue dogs are usually kept in someone's home, called a *foster home*, until a new home is found. Often the people in the foster home will improve the dog's training, housetraining, and health, depending on the dog's adoptability and needs.

Getting a dog from rescue is terrific. Because the dog lives with them, the people taking care of him end up knowing far more about that dog's temperament and needs than shelters typically can provide. Rescue folks may be able to tell you if the dog likes some cats but not others, that he chews tennis balls or hard toys into soggy shards, or if he jumps up on the furniture when no one is looking or when everyone is sitting on the couch. They will most likely be able to give you an idea of how well the dog fits into a group of dogs and if he guards his food and toys. Most importantly, they will be able to give you an overall idea of how well this dog does in a home. The only difficult aspect is that, because most rescues are run by fanciers of a specific breed, there aren't that many mixed breeds available.

Most rescue groups will ask you a lot of questions and make you fill out a lengthy form prior to considering your adoption. The rescue group doesn't want the dog to be returned and have yet another upheaval in his life. They will ask for references from friends and usually from a veterinarian. They will ask for such information as:

- Do you own or rent? If your rent do you have your landlord's permission?

- Do you have a fenced yard?
- How many people are in your home? What ages?
- Have you had dogs before?
- Where will the dog be when you're not home?
- Who will be the primary caretaker?
- What other pets do you have?
- Have you ever surrendered a pet before?
- How will you transport the pet?
- Can you afford veterinary fees?

Each group will have its own form, and the questions depend on the group's preferences. Don't be offended by the questions. They are for the benefit of the dog. The rescue groups want assurance that you can provide a good home.

Newspaper Ads

Classified ads in newspapers often advertise mixed breeds for sales, both puppies and adults. Mixed-breed puppies result from both planned and unplanned matings, but mostly the latter. The price should be minimal, although the days of "free to a good home" are gone, because many puppies will have already been taken to a vet, and the new owner will be expected to share that expense.

What's in a Name?

According to Mixed Breed Dog Club of America, "a Mixed Breed is the offspring of two different purebreds. The mating of a purebred and a mixed breed results in a litter of Mongrels. And, if both parents are either mixed breeds or mongrels, the pups are Mutts."

Rescues often take in dogs that show characteristics of a purebred, like this Basset Hound mix.

Before you take home the dog in question, ask as many questions as you can. The people may not know about the puppies' heritage, particularly if their dog just got out one day and came home pregnant. But it's also possible that an intact male jumped a fence into their back yard to get to the female in heat, in which case they may have seen your puppy's father.

Pet Stores

Many pet stores have adoption events from all-breed rescue groups or shelters in which both mixed breeds and purebreds are available. Some days puppies can be found at these events, sometimes it's just adults, because it depends on who the rescue group happens to have in foster homes. Some of these groups to go the same pet store every weekend, or on a regular schedule, in the hopes of finding a dog's forever home. Some pet stores sell mixed-breed dogs in a manner similar to a shelter. They can be great resources for mixed breeds.

Each rescue group or shelter will have its own procedures and requirements for adoption, but it's unlikely that you will walk into the store, fall in love, and walk out that afternoon with the dog.

Breeders

You wouldn't normally think of going to a breeder for a mix, but there are instances when it could happen. First, you may be looking for a specific cross (designer dog), and want to find a good breeder. And sometimes, even responsible breeders make mistakes, and unexpected litters happen. Because these unexpected mixed-breed puppies are considered to be of less value on the open market, they are typically either given away for free, sold for the cost of vet care they've had, or sold for a small fee that is far less than the value of a purebred.

If you decide you really must have a Peke-a-Poo, buy the dog from someone who knows what they're doing. Ask for health clearances, ask if the parents are on-site and ask to see them, ask for references from previous buyers, and ask if the breeder will take the dog back within its lifetime for any reason whatsoever. You have every right to get the same level of care and preparation as you would if you were buying a purebred.

With responsible breeders, you are not just buying the puppy, you are buying into a life-long relationship of assistance and advice,

Rescue Me!

Purebred clubs have rescue groups that take in unwanted dogs of their breed, which they then get healthy and adopt out for a fee to a good home. Some of these rescue groups take in mixed breeds who show a large percentage of the breed in question. Most of these folks go to shelters to rescue purebreds and will often see a mix they "spring" out of the shelter.

Health Clearances

Just because some designer dogs are popular doesn't mean that the breeder should make money hand over fist without providing any value for what you get. If you ask the Labradoodle breeder you're talking to about health clearances and the breeder says, "I don't do that stuff because I know my dogs are healthy," do *not* buy a puppy from that person under any circumstance; she is not a breeder so much as a retailer. It's irresponsible to breed dogs without doing every possible health clearance as part of the effort to produce healthy puppies.

if needed. A responsible breeder will ask you a lot of questions, most of which are similar to what a rescue group will ask (see above). They are not being nosy—they are simply trying to make certain that their puppy will have a good home.

If a designer-dog producer sells puppies on the Internet, and her main focus seems to be accepting credit cards for your deposit, not asking about what kind of home you can provide, *run away*. Do not buy from such a source; you will most likely end up with a problem dog. Expect the same things you would expect from a responsible purebred breeder, except the registration papers.

If you have your heart set on a designer dog like this Schnoodle, make sure that you find a good breeder.

Puppy Mills: The Sad Reality

Given the popularity of designer dogs, mixed breeds can now be found at puppy mills. A *puppy mill* is an unethical commercial breeder who has multiple breeds of dogs, with many puppies available almost all the time; the dogs are usually bred as soon as they are able to become pregnant again. The dogs are not socialized or cared for medically, and they have usually have little interaction with people, causing behavior problems down the road. In some puppy mills, breeding dogs are kept in tiny, filthy quarters.

Do not buy from puppy mills: If you

do, you are sending an economic signal that it's acceptable to you for someone to be cruelly neglectful to dogs. Don't kid yourself— puppy mills are as bad as you've heard, if not worse. Dogs from puppy mills generally have significant health and temperament problems related to the environment because they lacked hygiene, medical care, socialization of all types, and human attention. Signs of a puppy mill include:

- The place is dirty.
- They breed several breeds, both purebred and mixed.
- There are lots and lots of dogs living in outbuildings or a barn.
- The seller doesn't care if you will provide a good home and thus doesn't ask any questions.
- The seller only cares about payment, particularly cash.
- They push you to take a puppy that is only five weeks old, far too young to be separated from his mother. The puppy should be at least eight weeks old before he's allowed to go home with you.
- They have puppies available almost all the time, instead of once or twice a year.

Some puppy mills strive to look like a reasonable commercial breeder and have nice web sites to deflect the realities of their operation. Listen to your gut instinct. If something feels wrong, don't buy—find another source. You will live with this dog for next 10 to 15 years, so spend as much effort as necessary to find a dog you want to live with for that long.

Designer Dogs at Bargain Prices

If you want a crossbreed of two purebred dogs, go to the shelter or look in the newspaper and pay a little bit of money. Designer dogs are showing up in shelters across the country, along with the other mixed breeds and many purebreds, so there's no need to spend big bucks.

TEMPERAMENT TESTING

Since no one gets a mixed breed for looks or conformation, the most important considerations are temperament and health. You can only get a general idea of health, even if you have the dog examined by a veterinarian, but you can certainly get a good idea of temperament, which is the single most important consideration in a pet.

Temperament testing is a method of determining how a dog reacts to certain stimulus; trained people, such as behaviorists and shelter workers, can determine through temperament testing if a dog is aggressive, playful, good with children and cats, or is inappropriate for a particular home. A Golden Retriever/American Staffordshire Terrier mix is going to want to play with balls, but until you meet the dog in person and conduct temperament tests, you won't know if that particular puppy has inherited the sunny Golden disposition or the feisty-but-sweet terrier disposition. (You can bet he'll have a lot of energy when young!)

Temperament Tests for Puppies

Many versions of puppy temperament tests are available, so do a little research and find one that makes sense to you or one that a trainer recommends. People who want dogs for performance competitions, such as agility or obedience, need to thoroughly test an individual dog to see how trainable he is. For pet owners, it's best to find a dog with a temperament in the middle ground: not aggressive, not timid, confident but not overconfident.

When you select the puppy from the shelter, rescue, breeder, or other source, try hard not to be swayed by your kid's preference for the cute but fearful puppy who has a black spot over his eye. He'll probably be a less well-adjusted dog than the more confident, trainable puppy who isn't quite as cute. It's tough to say no to your kids, but getting an appropriate temperament in a family dog is critical.

Each professional's test is different. In Volhard's, each category

Puppy Test

Trainer Wendy Volhard has an excellent temperament test for puppies that can be found on the Internet at www. volhard.com.

Don't be enticed by a puppy's adorable face—make sure that his temperament will work with your family.

A shelter will do temperament testing for possession aggression.

is scored differently, with about six ratings to determine such characteristics as the level of pack drive, prey drive, sensitivity to touch, or level of fight or flight response. Your goal is to find a temperament in the middle range, and not on the far edge of either dominance or submission. You want a confident, friendly, trainable dog.

It's best if someone who is professionally knowledgeable about dogs conducts the tests, but you can read about it and conduct your own without undue worry. If this will be your first dog (congratulations!), bring along a friend who has experience. The tests listed here are quite general.

Confidence: Place the puppy a few feet away from you and clap your hands loudly. Aggressive puppies will come over with a tail up and try to bite your moving hands. The independent puppy won't come over. A shy puppy will hesitate for a while before coming over. A confident puppy will come over immediately or soon without being aggressive or fighting the other puppies.

Your Leadership: Walk away from the puppy but encourage him to follow you; call to him, make hand movements, pretend to run away. The more aggressive puppy gets underfoot and might try to bite your feet. The independent one won't follow. The confident one will follow with his tail up. A submissive puppy will urinate or not move toward you.

Restraint: Roll the puppy on his back and hold him there for 30 seconds. The more dominant dogs struggle mightily. An independent pup doesn't move much and avoids eye contact with you. The confident pup will settle down after a few moments. The submissive dog will roll right onto his back with no problem, and possibly urinate. This test indicates how submissive the dog is; dominant dogs need experienced owners, and these guys are not the best choice for beginners.

Dominance: If you want to participate in obedience trials, this test is critical, because the more dominant dogs may refuse to obey. Sit the puppy in front of you and stroke him from head to tail while keeping your head low enough for him to lick. A dominant puppy will growl, a very submissive one will roll over, an independent one wants to get away. A confident puppy accepts petting from you and also licks your face.

Sound Sensitivity: A strong reaction to a loud noise indicates fear and shyness. While the puppy is not facing you, make sudden sharp noise by dropping a metal pan on noncarpeted floor. Aggressive puppies will walk to the bowl and bark at it. The dog who backs off is fearful and timid (submissive). The puppy who walks toward the sound is confident.

Touch Sensitivity: Squeeze gently between the toes of a front foot with your fingers and gradually increase the pressure. Stop when the puppy shows discomfort. Training is easier with dogs who show sensitivity.

Temperament tests are useful for determining what basic personality a dog has. Don't forget, though, that environment shapes temperament, too. Both nature and nurture factor into how a puppy will behave as an adult.

Temperament Tests for Adults

Most shelters use a temperament test created by Sue Sternberg or Emily Weiss. Wherever you get your adult mix, the employees should have conducted some level of temperament testing that includes:

- How social is the dog?
- How comfortable is he with being touched?
- How comfortable is he when food is taken away?
- How does he react when toys or a bone is taken away?
- What is the dog's reaction with unfamiliar people?
- How does he react to children?
- How does he act with other dogs?
- How aroused or excited does he get?
- If his arousal is high, does he use his mouth or jump up?
- What is the dog's basic trainability? Has he had any basic training?
- Is he cat friendly? (Cat compatibility tests are usually on request; if you have a cat, you definitely want to ask.)

Strays

If you find a stray, either bring him in to your shelter, or, at the least, let them know you have this stray. "Be extremely conservative in your interaction with this stray," says canine behavior consultant Chelse Wieland. "Don't introduce a stray to your pets, not only for behavior reasons but also for disease prevention. Be particularly cautious if you have children. Strays can be a loaded bomb because you know nothing about the dog. You can go back the shelter and find out if this dog would be a good match after they have temperament tested and you know something about the dog."

How to Register Your Mixed Breed

Yes, you can register a mixed breed! You just can't register him with the American Kennel Club. The American Canine Hybrid Club (ACHC) and the Mixed Breed Dog Club of America (MBDCA) are both registries for mixed-breed dogs.

As a dog club and registry, MBDCA provides registration through membership, as they are essentially one and the same. A neuter or spay certificate for each dog and a fee are required to join. It allows your dog to work toward titles in obedience, tracking, retrieving, and lure coursing. The club certifies their own judges based on training, showing, and judging experience. It also offers a form of conformation, although certainly your dog is not expected to conform to a breed standard. The MBDCA conformation promotes happy, healthy family dogs, and thus emphasizes temperament, manners, and general soundness and balance—in other words, the title tells the world how well your dog conforms to the concept of a good family dog. The club emphasizes this point, since one of their goals is to promote responsible ownership of mixed breeds. Purebred dogs that cannot compete through the major purebred registries are also welcome in all programs except conformation. Disabled dogs, mixed or purebred, can also participate as long as you can provide a veterinarian's certificate indicating the dog is physically capable of doing the work involved. All dogs must be spayed or neutered before being registered with MBDCA.

Adolescence

According to canine behavior consultant Chelse Wieland, a dog isn't an adult until between the ages of two and three years. "There are a lot of changes between one and two-and-a-half," said Wieland. "Certain breeds mature faster, but for most dogs, adolescence ends after the age of two. We see a lot of physiological changes during adolescence, and we see changes in adolescent dogs."

But you shouldn't just rely on others to help determine an adult mix's temperament. Canine behavior consultant Chelse Wieland believes that the first thing to do, even before you meet the dog, is to ask as many questions as you can from whoever has the dog. Ask about his history, his interactions with people, other dogs, and children. You want to know, as much as possible, what type of situation this dog has been in, and what his behavior was like.

"One central question that is the most predictive component of behavior in a new house," says Wieland, "is 'what was the dog like in the previous household?' You can do food bowl tests and handling tests, which can be helpful, but what was the dog like before? If he was aggressive there, there's a higher chance he could be aggressive in the new house in a similar context. Also, find out how long the group has had the dog. If a group has only had a dog for a few days, his temperament is harder to measure as he's stressed and may not show his true colors."

Wieland's main advice is in regard to cautious dogs. "One common thing I hear frequently from clients is 'When I met him, he didn't want to approach me.' That's a critical concern, because the most common aspect of aggressive dogs is being cautious toward newcomers. Caution and suspicion can be problematic in adolescent and adult dogs."

Keep in mind that dogs are different in different contexts, and that's why you want to keep asking questions. Rehomed dogs go through a honeymoon period that last about three weeks; during the honeymoon, the dog is a bit anxious and on best behavior.

"If you have a one–year-old dog, you have the next year to find out who they're going to become and help influence them as well," says Wieland. "In an adult dog, you have three to six months to learn about who they are and how they're going to react in most contexts and environments. That's the tough thing; they can do great in one setting and not well at another, and vice versa: They can do better in a different setting than the one they're in. Just seeing the dog in a foster home doesn't mean the dog will be the same in the next household."

If you're looking into adopting an adult, Wieland encourages people to find a professional who might be able to give guidance about whether or not it's a good match, such as a behaviorist or someone in a shelter's behavior department. Lots of people ask behaviorists about this during a phone consultation; you tell the behaviorist what is known about the dog, what your situation is, and the behaviorist can tell you if it sounds like a good match, or why it doesn't. Some shelters have a professional behaviorist go with the person to meet the dog and do a temperament test.

HOME PREPARATION

Set your puppy up for success by being prepared for him before he gets to your home. If it's possible, avoid bringing him home

Decide in advance where your dog will sleep.

during times such as holidays, family reunions, or anything that involves your household being busier and more crowded than usual. However, if you plan to spend a holiday at home doing nothing but hanging out with your new dog, then a holiday can be a terrific time to get a new dog. You don't have to work, and you can devote your holiday to getting to know your puppy. But unless you plan to stay home and not have company, holidays like Christmas or Hanukkah are too busy to be a reasonable time to bring home a new

You'll have to decide on some rules for your dog: Will he be allowed on the couch or on your bed?

dog.

Even though you've been waiting for your dog for what feels like forever, he's bound to have more concerns than you do. You've planned for this—he hasn't, and tiny puppies have no idea what is happening. Your puppy just left his mother and siblings, and walked into a scary strange place where nothing is familiar. He will need company in the beginning, and will most likely not enjoy being alone at first because he's never been alone before. Give your puppy some reassurance, and let him acclimate in his own time. If your new arrival is an adult, he may need a little more down time and privacy than a puppy while he adjusts to such a major change.

Before the puppy walks in the door, decide who in the family is going to be responsible for what chores: who feeds him, who walks him, who housetrains him. If there are only two of you, it's easy to divide tasks, but tasks are also easy to overlap by accident. If you have five family members, make sure the dog doesn't get five breakfasts (housetraining a constantly full puppy would be a serious challenge).

Small children are always extremely excited at the puppy's arrival, so make sure their excitement doesn't frighten the puppy. The screams that toddlers tend to make can frighten already nervous puppies. Show your children how to pick up the puppy, when to leave him alone, to not touch him when he's in his crate, and so on. Being dropped accidentally can cause a dog to be nervous forever about being picked up and held. Show your kids how you expect them to treat the puppy.

Also decide in advance where the puppy is going to sleep, and if you're going to crate train. Will he sleep in his crate? Do you want a crate for upstairs and downstairs? Have all the dog's supplies there when he arrives, such as the crate, his own bed, food and water bowls, and a couple of toys.

Puppy-Proofing Your Home

Small children and puppies are quite a bit alike: For one thing, they experience the world through their mouths. Both toddlers and puppies will put any manner of items in their mouths, such as car keys, bookmarks, caviar, and shoelaces. Help your dog by removing any items that could be dangerous or that you definitely don't want to lose, like those expensive new shoes or leather jacket. If your collection of glass figurines can be reached by teeth and paws, and are located on the bottom shelf of a display cabinet without a glass covering, put them somewhere else until your puppy is trustworthy. Put them away completely, like in a box in the back of a closet.

Just like baby-proofing a house, you want to get things out of

Before you bring your pup home, make sure that your house is puppy proofed.

his level that you know will interest him. It doesn't take much to attract the attention of a curious puppy who wants to pop whatever he sees into his mouth. Besides keeping your stuff safe, it's important that your puppy not start out life with emergency surgery during which the vet extracts a toenail clipper from his belly (in technical veterinary terms, that's a foreign obstruction).

Potentially hazardous cleaning materials, such as bleach or ammonia, shouldn't stay in a floor-level cabinet. Move them temporarily until the puppy is older or put child-proof locks on cabinet doors (which you can

You mixed breed will enjoy having a dog bed to relax in.

also use on some closet doors). Keep the carpet cleaner and urine odor remover in an easily accessible place, though, because you'll definitely need those.

Think about basic safety. Keep garbage under tight cover, or outside, or up; trash hounds can get pancreatitis or some of those infamous foreign obstructions. Close doors to rooms you don't want the puppy to explore. Use a pet or child safety gate to block off stairs. Electrical cords, particularly those huge clumps behind entertainment centers or computers, can be taped together or pulled up off the floor.

The First Night Home

Young puppies who have just left all they have ever known are facing the longest night of their lives. You wouldn't be your normal cheerful self if you'd just lost your family and had no idea what's going to happen next, or who you're going to be with. Some dogs will see it as an adventure. Some will just wonder what that car ride was all about—all that motion and noise and those strangers may have made the puppy's stomach upset.

Make this first night as easy as possible for your puppy and let him sleep in your bedroom, in a crate or on his own dog bed placed near your bed. He can hear you, smell you, see you, and know that he is not alone. Putting him in a room by himself will only increase his worry, and you'll hear him all night. Besides, if he's sleeping near you, you'll have a good idea of when he needs to go out; if it's been a while since you've had a puppy, you'll need to take him outside more often than you remember the last puppy having to go out. This advice also is appropriate for an adult's first night in a new home.

Bed Tip

While many dog beds are selected because they are attractive, don't forget to consider how easy it is to wash when you buy one.

Sleeping in Your Bed?

Unless your dog is quite dominant, it won't ruin his temperament to sleep in your bed with you. He's either a dominant dog or he isn't, and sleeping in your bed isn't going to make a submissive dog turn dominant. (You don't want the dominant dog to sleep in your bed because it gives him an exalted sense of his place in the household.)

One concern about having the puppy sleep there the first night is, rather obviously, that he hasn't yet been fully housetrained. Even a trained adult dog may be awfully nervous that first night and have problems controlling his bladder. The other concern is that, if the dog is only eight weeks old, you don't really know yet how dominant he's going to be. It's far better to allow the dog to sleep with you later on as a privilege, rather than to take away something he has come to perceive as his right.

So, while it's not a good idea for a young puppy to sleep in your bed on the first night, it is all right later when he's housetrained. No matter where the dog sleeps, though, he needs to know that he has his own space, which he doesn't have to share with anyone (preferably his crate).

Dog-Proofing Your Yard

It's unfortunate that many new home communities do not allow fencing in their neighborhoods, because it is the one tool that will keep your dog safer than anything else. It keeps him at home, off the streets where cars travel, and away from loose dogs. The fence keeps your dog inside a specific perimeter, unless he's a digger. Many dogs, particularly dachshund and terrier mixes, have the potential to dig. For those dogs who like to dig, it's necessary to check the perimeter of the fence on a regular basis and block the holes that have been started. It's quite a jolt to look out your front window and see your dog running off joyfully and unattended, right in front of a car.

You can find matching collars and leashes for your fashionable mix.

Electronic fences work through wires buried underground; your dog wears an attachment on his collar that gives a small electric shock if he crosses over the wire. These fences are not ideal, because they do not keep out people, dogs, or wildlife. Some dogs, particularly dominant ones, don't care about the imposed restraints and just run through the invisible barrier. If your dog runs to get away from another dog who has entered your fence perimeter, your dog will either be cornered or zapped. Also, the electronic ding that makes the fence effective can cause some sensitive dogs to be fearful; some of these dogs can have an unwelcome temperament change as a result of being zapped. However, in some communities where private fences are not allowed, an electronic fence is better than having no fence at all.

BASIC SUPPLIES

Before you bring your mix home, make sure that you purchase some basic supplies. Most can be found at any pet supply store.

Bed

Even if your dog sleeps with you in your bed, he will still enjoy having his own dog bed (or two or three, strewn about the house for convenience and accessibility). Even the most people-oriented mixes like to nap quietly by themselves sometimes. If too much activity is going on in the house, or if he doesn't feel well, he may like a bed of his own.

Read the labels before you buy the bed; manufacturers often use fabrics that are supposed to be washed in cold water. (Perhaps bed manufacturers don't own dogs and have no clue what dogs actually do in there.) Dogs chew treats, pass gas, shred toys, shed, puke, and sometimes have accidents (particularly puppies and seniors). Ear or eye ointment can get on the bed when the dog wipes his face on it. Dirt from outside comes in on feet that go directly to that bed. Buy a bed that you can wash in warm water; it just makes sense.

Collar and Leash

A collar and leash are quite necessary for your dog. Puppies should have a soft, adjustable buckle collar. Select a lightweight one made of nylon so that there isn't much weight on the dog's neck. Chain link collars are too heavy for puppies. Choosing between nylon or leather collar for adults is a matter of personal preference, because both work well.

You should be able to slip two fingers underneath the collar at all times; check a puppy's collar frequently, because puppies grow so quickly that he may need a bigger collar or two sooner than you expect.

Slip (choke) collars are used by some trainers, but these collars are best left to professionals—most people do not use them correctly. They are not used by positive-reinforcement trainers

Crate Use

Don't overuse your crate, or you'll be creating as many problems as you'd hoped to solve. Crates are great training tools, but no dog can tolerate being in one all day while you're at work, home for dinner, gone to a movie, and then at night for sleep. That's far too much time in a crate. Some dogs who are crated far too much for far too long end up with some obsessive/compulsive behaviors.

because choke collars use physical discomfort to train. Used incorrectly, choke or prong collars can harm a dog's neck.

Depending on whether you have a toy breed mix or Great Dane/St. Bernard mix, your puppy can use a leash that is 4 or 6 feet (1 or 2 m) in length. With giant-sized mixes, you may as well start out with the 6-foot (2 m) leash. For training classes, a leather leash is best, but for home, you can have one of those cute, whimsical nylon webbing leashes. Chain link leashes are too heavy for most puppies.

Replace your leash every few years, especially if your dog chews it or pulls hard. If the leash breaks while you're walking an excited dog, mayhem can result!

Crate

Crating can make life easier for you and safer for your puppy. A crate offers a puppy a place to call his own. Many people with lots of dogs feed their dogs in crates, partly to reinforce that good things occur inside the crate, but mostly to keep the dogs separated during meals. Crates can be very useful in housetraining—as long as they are not overused—because dogs try to avoid soiling where they sleep.

Crates make your life simpler by offsetting "puppy hurricanes." Whether your mix is small or large, don't underestimate the damage a small curious puppy can cause. Crates can help avoid the horror stories of puppies tearing up couches, eating rugs, and swallowing various items out of the laundry basket.

Besides, using crates for traveling, either to agility events or your father's house, makes life easy both on the road and when you arrive. Your dog always has a safe, familiar place to be. Crates are also useful for recuperating from surgery—as long as the dog is used to the crate before the surgery. You can't just slam a post-surgical dog who hasn't been adjusted to one into a crate—it could increase his stress.

Ceramic or stainless steel food bowls are good choices for your dog.

Crates come in a variety of sizes and styles; while you want your adult dog to be able to stand up in it and turn around, a larger crate doesn't help housetrain as well as one sized for a puppy. If you choose to buy only one, buy an adjustable one that should eventually fit the adult dog. Knowing what size a mixed-breed puppy will turn out to be, however, can be problematic in terms of buying a crate.

First-Aid Kit

No one ever expects anything bad to happen, but when an emergency occurs, being prepared can save your dog's life. This kind of preparation is assisted by getting in touch with your inner type-A personality, because those characteristics really shine when it comes to prevention.

You can buy a pet first-aid kit or make your own. Some supplies in a human first-aid kit, like tape or ibuprofen, are not going to work well for most dogs (ibuprofen shouldn't be used for dogs, although you can use a small amount of aspirin). If you make one yourself, buy a pet first-aid book and place it in the kit so that you're not looking for it when there is an emergency.

Basic supplies include vet wrap, gauze pads, scissors, tweezers, iodine, triple antibiotic ointment, antiseptic towelettes, and eye wash. If you go hiking or camping, be sure to take supplies with you. See Chapter 8 for more details on first aid.

Food and Water Bowls

Bowls for your mix come in several materials. Metal or ceramic bowls are best because the plastic ones tend to harbor bacteria. Also, dogs can chew plastic bowls but they can't chew ceramic ones.

Clean these bowls with dishwashing soap after every meal. Water bowls tend to get scummy from the water, and food bowls get greasy from the fat content in the food. It helps keep your feeding area clean to have a place mat or rug underneath the two bowls. Some dogs are so messy that it doesn't make much difference, and some dogs are so neat that food or water never goes on the floor.

Grooming Supplies

All dogs need grooming; some just need more of it than others. Short-coated mixes, such as a Boxer/Dalmatian mix, will shed a lot,

Toenail Issues

Many dogs have issues with their toenails, and they don't like to have them touched, much less trimmed. Some dogs equate this with the end of the world. If you give in to a dog's dislike of having his toes touched, much less fondled, you are looking at a lifetime of toenail angst. If you get your mixed breed as a puppy, touch all of his toes with your hands and expose them to the toenail trimmer. Play with his feet by kissing his toes, holding individual toes, and so on, to acclimate him to the reality that his toes will be touched whether he likes it or not. See Chapter 5 for more on grooming your mix.

but they can be groomed with a hound glove. Dogs with hair that grows and does not shed, like Schnauzer or Poodle mixes, will need professional grooming at least occasionally but will also need brushing with a slicker brush. Long-coated dogs, such as Newfoundland, Golden, and Border Collie mixes need to be brushed with either a pin brush or a bristle brush. Grooming supplies depend on the type of coat your mixed breed has.

See Chapter 5 for a complete list of grooming equipment, but the basics include a wire slicker brush, metal comb, trimming scissors, nail trimmers, and styptic powder or pen.

Identification

Adult rescues who are new to a home are prone to bolt out an open door. Watching your dog take off like lightning can be a terrifying experience, with devastating results. Sometimes, no matter how careful you are, even if you live alone, your dog can get out. Determined dogs will figure a way out, and some dogs will just take advantage of a moment when the door is open and you're asking the letter carrier what happened to that magazine.

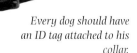

Every dog should have an ID tag attached to his collar.

Be prepared in case the unexpected happens. Always have identification on your dog. There are several ways to ID him if he's out bounding around with the neighborhood fellows, whooping it up and having a good time while you drive around the neighborhood craning your neck and missing stop signs.

Tags

Every dog should have an ID tag with your phone number and street address attached to his collar. Some people also put their names on the tag and add a work or cell phone number; some even swear by the promise of a "reward" written on the tag. Certain municipalities require that a dog wear an ID tag with a rabies tag and city license. Although ID tags can fall off, or the whole collar can be removed, it's still inexpensive insurance that can assist in a quick return home.

Microchipping

Microchipping is a high-tech way to ID your dog. Your veterinarian injects a chip, about the size of a grain of rice, between your dog's shoulder blades with what is essentially a big syringe. No local anesthesia is needed. The microchip has a number that pops up on a computer screen when scanned. This number corresponds to a database with your name and address.

If your dog is ever lost, shelters or vet offices can scan him, call the database, and find you. Voila! However, remember to update the database information if you move or change phone numbers.

There are different types of scanners, and not all can read every type of microchip. So while the chip can't be lost, without the correct scanner, it's useless. A microchip is an additional tool that goes with an ID tag but does not replace it. However, a dog who is microchipped still has a better chance of being returned home than one who isn't.

Safety Gates

Safety gates are designed to keep pets (and kids) from falling down stairs and going into rooms you don't want them in. With safety gates, you can block off a room but still see into it. Conversely, you can keep your dog in a specific room rather than out of one. One common use for safety gates is to block access to a cat's litter box, preventing inappropriate rummaging for snacks—anything you can do to prevent your dog from getting into the litter box is a great idea.

Some gates are simple, and some have more complicated features. Several are short and are attached by temporary pressure mounting that can be altered; some are kept in one place permanently with hardware mounting. A few are designed to cover wide doorways that don't have doors. Some gates even have cat doors, so that your cat can go in a room and your dog can't. Safety gates are sold at both pet supply stores and children's supply or toy stores.

Toys

Toys are necessary—not optional—supplies, particularly when your puppy is teething and the only thing he wants is to relieve his jaw discomfort by chewing on something. To ensure that he's not chewing something inappropriate (like your mother-in-law's shoes), get him some toys. Get a lot of toys and leave a few of them out. Then exchange those

Find safe, size-appropriate toys for your dog.

toys with others so that your dog feels like there's something new to pique his interest. That said, don't leave out a hundred toys, because having too many to choose from is almost as bad as not having any.

Keep safety in mind. If the toy is plush with a squeaker, get rid of it once your dog has disemboweled it. Once the outer portions of it are shredded, such as the tail, mane, ears, and tail of a giraffe, keep an eye on the seams. Once it breaks apart, toss it, so the filling or the squeaker won't be ingested. Some dogs need hard toys to chew, and those are often in the form of hard plastic. Keep an eye on your dog's teeth if he likes to chew hard toys, and remove the toy if you detect a dental problem.

Don't ride with your dog loose in the car; he's much safer in a crate or with a doggy seatbelt attachment.

Toys help puppies develop into adults. Play translates into practice for real life. Play fighting, hunting, chasing, disemboweling, shredding, and so on help puppies grow up. Playing with toys helps develop muscle tone and creativity, and also helps teach mouth inhibition, which every puppy needs to learn. Chasing after balls improves a puppy's motor skills. Plus, playing with your dog by throwing a toy for him is a good bonding method. In addition to bonding, because you are in control of the games, you reinforce your status as leader.

ON THE ROAD: TRAVELING WITH YOUR MIX

Many people like to hop in the car with their dog rather than leave him at home. Dogs usually make good traveling companions, as long as you use common sense and are adequately prepared. If you're staying at a friend's or relative's house, make absolutely certain your dog is welcome; showing up with a dog can be awkward if they don't like dogs or won't let them in the house. (Incredibly, some people don't let dogs inside the house, even unbelievably cute, well-behaved dogs who wouldn't chew anything or pee on the carpeting.) If your dog is allowed to visit, make sure he doesn't bother anyone by barking, stealing food, doing a little gardening, or annoying the cat who lives there.

Check a travel guide to see which motels or hotels accept dogs. Sometimes just knowing that a certain hotel chain allows pets makes your travel plans easier. Places that accept dogs usually indicate that on their signs. Make sure you keep your dog under good control, clean up after him, and don't leave him alone in the motel room if he's going to bark his head off. Cleaning up after him, whether it's his feces or his hair, is your responsibility, not the motel's. Hang out the "do not disturb" sign so that employees don't open the room door and accidentally let the dog out.

Riding in the Car

Many people keep their dogs in crates while in the car to keep them safe. A crate contains your dog in event of an accident, and also keeps him in one spot rather than allowing him to hop back and forth between the front seat or get his head caught from stepping on the power window button.

Some people prefer a doggie seat belt, in which the dog's safety belt is threaded around the car's seat belt. Your dog is always safest in the back seat, but if your car has air bags, it is *essential* to keep

Be sure to pack your dog's leash when you travel.

Cleansers: A Puppy Owner's Other Best Friend

Spot removers for pets are meant to remove the spots dogs leave when they throw up or pee or poop inside. For some reason, dogs consider brand new carpeting and rugs to be a terrific place for these activities. Some dogs will use the same spot in the same room for years, ruining that carpeting and leaving no other option than to replace it. The better your cleanser is at removing specific urine and feces odors, the longer your carpeting or rug will last.

White vinegar is good with urine spots on rugs and floors, but it's not quite strong enough for carpets. Get a product specifically designed for spot cleaning carpeting, as well as something enzymatic that will really kill the scent. If the scent of urine, feces, or vomit is still in the carpeting after you've cleaned it, the dog will return to the "scene of the crime" repeatedly. If you can managed to truly eradicate the scent right away, you'll have less trouble. That goes for spots on carpeting, tile, or hardwood floor, or in a corner. Once the padding below the carpeting is ruined, it's almost impossible to get dogs to stop peeing in that same spot unless you pull up the carpeting and replace that bit of padding.

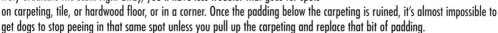

the dog in the back seat.

On a long trip, stop every couple of hours for a quick potty break. The motion of the car may make your dog need to go more often, and stretching legs is as good for you as it is for him. Bring water from home or buy bottled water so that he doesn't get a digestive upset from a change in water.

Although it seems quite obvious not to leave your dog alone inside a car when it's hot, it happens regularly. Every summer, dogs go into heat distress or even die because they are left alone in a hot car. Inside a car with closed windows, the temperature can shoot up to dangerous heights quickly. Dogs can have problems just while you're in the grocery store getting milk. Even if you crack the windows, temperatures inside a car can reach a fatal 120°F (38.8°C) in minutes. It's a preventable disaster. Conversely, if you're driving in winter, you can leave the dog in the car alone for a few minutes, but not too much longer.

Flying

Every airline has its own regulations about pet travel and, even within individual airlines, the regulations change regularly. Check with the airline before you make the reservation, and again a few days before you fly to see if anything has changed. Ask the airline

Don't let your dog get lost when you travel— keep your eye on him at all times.

what is required, and parrot it back to them. Few things are more frustrating in this world than missing a flight because you haven't followed the airline's rules.

Ask what kind of crates and paperwork they require. Typically, airlines accept plastic-sided crates with handles for carrying, but not wire or fabric crates for use in cargo. The crate should have enough room so that your dog can stand up and turn around; dogs who otherwise have everything necessary have been declined for flight because the crate isn't big enough. Place absorbent material on the bottom. On the outside of the crate, put a Live Animal and This End Up sticker, and something showing your contact information (with the phone number at which you can be reached after the flight), the destination, and a cell phone number if you have one. Typically, a health certificate signed by a veterinarian is needed that has been issued within 10 days of travel and a current rabies certificate.

Tiny mixes can accompany you in the cabin, and some airlines allow soft-sided carriers for on-board use. Soft-sided carriers adjust well under the seat in front of you where the dog must stay during the flight. (You are not allowed to take the dog out of the carrier.) Be sure to ask the airline in advance what type of carrier is acceptable for in-cabin use.

GOING OUT OF TOWN

It's sad but true: Sometimes you must leave your dog at home while you go out of town. While there are many vacations on which your dog can accompany you, it's hard to take him to Aunt Thelma's funeral or to a corporate-wide meeting.

Kennels

As with finding a veterinarian, spend some time looking for pet care before you need it. If your vet clinic doesn't board, ask them for a kennel recommendation. People seem to dislike the idea of a boarding kennel more than dogs do, because most dogs think of it as a camping trip, not a concentration camp. One way to start rating a kennel is to ask if it is accredited with the American Boarding Kennels Association (ABKA).

Ask for a tour of the area in which your dog would stay; if they say you can't go back there, leave, find another kennel, and don't look back. There is no reason they should keep you from seeing that area, other than wanting to hide conditions you won't like. Kennels should appear clean and dry, and the dogs should look relatively relaxed. Of course, some dogs will never be completely relaxed in a kennel, but as long as you can see that the kennel is clean and well maintained, and the people are friendly with the dogs, it should be all right. You can all the Better Business Bureau to see if any complaints have been filed.

Pet Sitters

Professional pet sitters can be a terrific option when you go away, particularly if you have more than one or two pets, because kennels charge per pet per day. So do pet sitters, but it usually costs less, and your dog is in his own home and bed. Pet sitters should be bonded (legally trustworthy), insured, and have good references. They can stay at your house or drop by for a preassigned number of visits per day. If your dog has access to the back yard through a dog door, twice a day is fine.

There's also the option of hiring a house sitter—someone to stay in the house with your pets and make the house look lived in. Some people do this regularly for income; many vet techs do it for

If you can't bring your dog with you, a pet sitter might be the perfect answer.

the extra money. Young adults who are reliable can be good too, as long as they are responsible.

Friends

Perhaps your dog can stay at a friend's house. Make sure the person is knowledgeable about dogs and responsible enough to take care of your pet. This approach is appealing because the dogs are in a home, and it's usually free or a good deal, but friends aren't always as careful as you'd like them to be.

Whichever option you choose, make sure they understand your dog's needs and that any medications or medical problems must be taken care of appropriately. Be sure to leave them a way to contact you or a timeframe in which you will be checking in.

DOGGY DAYCARE

Who cares if your mother fell over laughing when you mentioned you might want to use doggy daycare for your beloved mix? Doggy daycare is growing rapidly in popularity because it makes sense in today's busy world. If you work long or irregular hours, live in an inclement climate, or have been ill yourself, doggy daycare is a great way for someone else to help get your dog exercised, stimulated, and socialized.

Like daycare for kids, all doggy daycares are not created equal—be careful in your selection of a facility. Get out and do some research by visiting the places available. Good doggy daycares only accept dogs who aren't aggressive and are able to play nice with other dogs. It would be an insane asylum if the facility was filled with dogs who didn't get along. This is one area in which daycare is quite different for kids than for dogs.

Before you select a doggy daycare, stop in to visit those in your area. The main concern is whether or not the dogs look stressed. Inevitably, there will be a dog or two having a stressful day, but if all of the dogs look overwhelmed and stressed, then it's best to stay away from that facility. As part or your research, ask if there is a limit on how many dogs are allowed at the facility during the business day. See if the facility looks clean, and if there are any dog messes left on the floor (accidents happen, but they should be cleaned up immediately). If there are both indoor and outdoor spaces, consider if both areas are large enough to accommodate all the dogs over the course of a given day. Talk to the employees to get a feel for how the place is run and how they handle the dogs. They don't have to be trainers, as long as whoever is in charge has experience with groups of dogs. Dog mentality changes when they're in a pack, and the employees should be familiar with that. With a little research, you can make the best choice and come from a long day at work to take home a dog who has already had a wonderful day and won't mind just crashing on the couch with you.

Finding a good team to help care for your dog while you're away will bring you peace of mind.

FEEDING

Your Mixed Breed

Dogs are omnivores. That means they will willingly eat just about anything, much like a goat will. They do not differentiate between edibility and digestibility. Dogs will eat whatever looks good to them, whether it is good for them or not. The odor of a given object has a lot to do with its appeal: Whoever would have thought that a decomposing rodent or a bottle of ear cleanser would have the appeal of a tasty treat? Cat food, garbage, pasta glued to a frame and sprayed with glitter, even other dogs' poop—your dog sees it all as part of one great big smorgasbord. You understand this when you hear laughter on the other end of the phone when you ask the Poison Control Center "Are disposable diapers toxic to ingest?" Your dog is not the first one to sample a used diaper.

In the arena of food, dogs do not think, they just eat. It's instinctual. When you adopt your mixed breed, you take on responsibility for him. You are the one in charge, and you must make sure that your dog eats a healthy diet. That means no junk food, no pizza, no fast food wrappers, and certainly no chocolate (save that for yourself). It means a balanced, nutritionally appropriate diet for the canine species.

READING THE LABEL

In the United States, pet food is regulated by the government. The Food and Drug Administration (FDA), the Association of American Feed Control Officials (AAFCO), and the U.S. Department of Agriculture all play a role in regulating dog food. Also, above and beyond the federal government, some states have feed and labeling laws.

AAFCO defines ingredients that can legally and appropriately be used in your dog's food. AAFCO also establishes nutrition profiles, conducts feeding trials to match food against nutritional needs, and is responsible for writing pet food regulations and then making sure those regulations are followed.

AAFCO has outlined appropriate nutrition for a canine diet, and it's up to the pet food manufacturers to make sure their food meets this definition. The manufacturers make sure they're up to snuff by conducting food trials—not just out of the goodness of their hearts, but because they have to.

Oddly enough, the legal requirements for pet food labeling are stricter than they are for human food labeling, which can work to your advantage. Learn how to read the label on pet food, just as you've learned to read it on human food.

Looking at Ingredients

Ingredients are listed on the label by weight, so if beef is the first item listed, the largest quantity of any ingredient in that product is beef. If the first ingredient listed is something like bone meal or corn gluten, it's not a high-quality food, and it's best to avoid it. Some manufacturers will "split" ingredients on the label—chicken, chicken meal, chicken by-products—in order to make it look like there is more chicken in there than there really is. Learn to read between the lines on the product label so you understand what actually is in the food.

Learning how to read dog food labels can help to ensure that your dog is getting a quality diet.

The word "flavoring" on a food package doesn't just mean the food has a particular flavor, it indicates the percentage of certain ingredients. If liver is the first ingredient on the pet food label's list, the food must have at least 3 percent liver. If the label says the food only has liver flavoring, then it only must have enough liver flavor for dogs to smell it. While any dog worth his salt can smell liver a mile away, that doesn't mean there is actual liver in that food. It could be a "liver perfume," so to speak. So, reading the label will tell you if the product has any actual liver in it. By-products, those ingredients we are loathe to think about, are the leftover parts of animals after the better parts have been taken for human food; the less by-products in a dog food, the better.

Have fresh water available to your dog, especially if you are outside on a hot day.

Frustratingly enough, caloric content—seemingly the most basic requirement on human food labels—is not necessary on pet foods, although it's possible to call the manufacturer and ask. Some manufacturers have calorie counts on their websites.

Guaranteed Analysis

US law requires commercial foods to have a "guaranteed analysis" on the label. The guaranteed analysis refers to the minimum or maximum values of given nutrients. This ensures that the pet food has a minimum level of ingredients most important to your dog's health, such as protein and fat, and a maximum of other materials, such as fiber and water. (Of course your dog needs fiber and water, it's just that he doesn't need that much.)

Complete and Balanced

What your mix needs is a high-quality food. Look on the label for the phrase "complete and balanced." Because of strict pet food regulations, manufacturers cannot make this claim if the food is not complete and balanced, so low-quality foods won't have it on the label.

Premium foods are complete and balanced. These higher-quality foods are more expensive than lower-quality ones, but consider the money you will save on veterinary bills. Good nutrition helps keep your mix healthy. Just as you wouldn't feel great on a diet of fast food, your dog will not be healthy on food made mostly of cereal

Water Is Life

The most critical nutrient of all, clean fresh water, should be available to your dog at all times. The only exception is when you're housebreaking a puppy and want him to have water only at scheduled times. But other than, free access is best for your dog.

Water is more important than food. A starving dog can keep going with only half the muscle mass he's supposed to have, but he will die if he loses a mere 15 percent of his body water. Dogs can survive longer without food than they can without water.

There's a not a lot of point in paying for premium dog food and regular vet visits if your dog's body will be affected daily by inappropriate contaminants in water. In some U.S. cities, tap water contains a lot of pollutants and/or chlorine; filter your dog's water, or buy distilled, to protect your dog from harmful water contaminants. Also, filtering can help prevent water-borne diseases, such as cryptosporidium, *Giardia*, leptospirosis, and *E. coli*.

fillers. One other plus—the protein in premium brands comes from better sources than the less expensive brands, which makes the food more digestible. This means (wonderfully!) that you have a bit less poop to clean up.

Of course, just because a food is complete and balanced and incredibly beneficial to your dog doesn't mean that he will like it. If your finicky eater finds a given food unpalatable, keep trying brands until you have a winner. While changing over, however, be sure to mix the food you are switching from with the food you are switching to for a few days to avoid unpleasant digestive upsets.

COMMERCIAL FOOD SELECTION

Now that you know how to read the label, what types of commercial foods are available for your mix?

The size of your mixed breed needs some consideration when selecting food. Toy-breed dogs should have food sized appropriately for their mouths, and preferably with some dental benefits because tiny dogs tend to have dental issues. Tiny dogs also have some metabolic concerns because of their size-to-body-weight ratio, and they may need as many calories as dogs twice their size; check with your veterinarian about caloric needs.

Dry Food

The most common choice of dog food is a commercially prepared kibble (dry food). Premium dry foods are complete and balanced, and wonderfully convenient. Lesser-quality kibble can have the nutritional equivalent of cardboard and sand, so read the label. Take some time to wander through the pet supply store, read the labels, and buy the best quality kibble you can afford.

There are many, many choices of kibble—varieties made specifically for puppies, adults, and seniors. Prescription foods that aid specific medical conditions, such as kidney problems, are available at your veterinarian's clinic. Some pet food companies make food with great nutrition and lousy taste appeal, while others make wonderful flavors that are the nutritional equivalent of the *Titanic*. Just because your dog loves a food doesn't mean it's good for him (just as many humans love junk food). However, you don't want to take away from your dog's quality of life by giving him, for years on end, a food that is not palatable. Enjoying food is critical to a dog's happiness, so keep experimenting until you find a good combination of nutrition and taste. Keep in mind that what tastes good to one dog may not taste as good to another. If you have more than one dog, it may be helpful, or even necessary, to have more than one brand of food in the house.

Most owners find dry food, or kibble, the most convenient food to feed their dogs.

Canned Food

Canned food is a bit like drugs for dogs: It can be addicting to the point of obsession. Like a chocolate sundae, canned dog food tastes great but is really fattening. It's easy for a dog to pig out on canned food. Other than the caloric content, however, it's fine nutritionally and has less added preservatives than kibble. There are valid reasons to use canned food: to appeal to finicky eaters, for toothless dogs, to increase water intake, to mix in medications, and to add weight to dogs who have been ill. It's not a good idea to feed nothing but canned food to a healthy dog; however, many dogs enjoy a blend of canned and kibble.

Semi-Moist Food

Just say no! Semi-moist food is the epitome of junk food. While it's okay as an occasional treat, it should not be the main nutritional base of your dog's diet. This stuff is full of sugar, salt, and other ingredients that aren't good for dogs. It's wonderfully convenient for traveling, but if your dog isn't used to it, he might get some gastrointestinal upset (which will defeat all the traveling convenience).

Prescription Foods

Your vet may advise a prescription diet if your dog has a specific medical condition that could be assisted by special food. Kidney troubles require a reduced-protein diet. Liver diseases require less sodium and protein. Diabetic dogs need a consistent amount of nutrition and more fiber than nondiabetics, because fiber helps lower the need for insulin. Gastrointestinal problems can be helped by food with high digestibility. Ill or recuperating dogs may need food with extra calories in order to heal properly. Many dogs being treated for cancer require some type of prescription food, depending on their treatment and medications. Not all medical problems require prescription food, and hopefully your dog will not need to remain on prescription food.

Do not simply choose out of the blue to give your dog a specialty diet—it is a decision you must make with your vet's advice. Prescription diet kibble is only available through veterinary clinics for good reason: This food is like medicine.

NON-COMMERCIAL DIETS

Some owners prefer to take the control of their dog's diet out of the hands of the manufactures and into their own kitchen.

Home-Cooked Diet

Cooking your dog's food is not as difficult as it sounds, and it can be an excellent alternative for dogs with food allergies. Because they are getting "real food" without additives, dogs on home-cooked diets tend to have beautiful glossy coats and good health. But the person doing to the cooking must understand basic canine nutrition. Getting the appropriate calcium/phosphorus ratio is particularly important for dogs. You must also avoid cooked bones, because these can splinter and rupture your dog's esophagus or intestines.

Home cooking is more time consuming and expensive than commercial diets, but if it appeals to you, do a little reading and talk to your vet. Some people cook for their dogs for medical reasons, some for overall health, and some simply because they want to. Whatever the reason, if home cooking is done properly, your dog will love you for it.

Raw Diet

Often referred to as the BARF, or biologically appropriate raw food diet, a raw food diet basically consists of raw meaty bones, chicken or beef parts, and pureed green leafy vegetables, (The vegetables are pureed to aid in their digestion.) Proponents of raw diets believe it is the most natural diet for dogs because it is what they would eat in the wild.

It can be complicated, so if you are considering starting this diet, do your research. You must learn how to provide the proper calcium/phosphorus ratio. Meat without the bones is insufficient, because calcium is in the bones, so you can't just feed raw hamburger.

Advantages to the diet include improved health and energy. Dental cleanings under anesthesia are usually unnecessary with this diet because the raw bones clean the teeth. Because there is no filler, the volume of feces is significantly smaller and the pieces disintegrate naturally and quickly outdoors, making cleanup easy and neat.

Those against this diet point out that the meat given to dogs on raw diets usually comes from a butcher, which isn't as natural as it would be in the wild. The butcher sells meat from animals that were given antibiotics and other drugs that wild animals wouldn't ever ingest. Dogs with impaired immune systems may be more prone to the bacteria in the food, such as *Salmonella,* which can make the dog ill. Also, this diet may be too rich for some dogs.

Before you embark upon feeding a raw diet, understand that it is quite controversial within the veterinary community because of the bacteria and parasites found in raw meat. Your veterinarian may give you a hard time about it or support you whole-heartedly. Do your research so you can make an informed decision about what's best for your dog.

Table Scraps

Even though table scraps are shared with the best of intentions and loving care, they are usually bad for dogs. They can have too

Vegetarian Diets

Dogs are not biologically suited to vegetarian diets. Although they are omnivores (they eat everything and anything), dogs need a certain amount of meat protein. Dogs on vegetarian diets can be sickly and unhealthy, and tend to have a lot of soft diarrhea.

much grease, fat, and spices for dogs to be able to digest without trouble. Your leftovers add up calories fast, and often the calories are empty (there is no scenario in the wild in which a dog would have the nutritional equivalent of pancakes and maple syrup). If your dog ends up preferring table scraps to his own dinner, you could be in for a long, stubborn battle of the wills.

FOOD ALLERGIES

If your dog has a food allergy, it will show up in his skin. Dogs with allergies don't get runny eyes and a stuffed up nose like people do; dogs get itchy skin problems. Food allergies commonly cause itching, sometimes severe. Signs of food allergies tend to be facial itching, chewing on feet, scratching the belly, or those frustrating recurrent ear infections. Food allergies don't just pop up overnight, but rather develop over a long period of time, usually years.

Beef, dairy, and wheat are common canine allergens. Unfortunately, most commercial foods tend to have a mixture of beef, dairy, wheat, lamb, fish, and chicken, so just changing brands will leave the dog still exposed to the same allergens. These dogs can try an unusual protein source, such as kangaroo, rabbit, or duck. Ask your vet about food in which the protein was predigested into bits too small to get the immune system involved; these are called *hydrolyzed proteins*. These hydrolyzed-protein

Food Safety

Just like any human food, pet food can be contaminated, despite the best efforts of the manufacturer. Food poisoning is a problem for pets just as it is for people.

Once in a while, you'll hear on the news about a pet food recall. In most cases where a recall is initiated, the most common culprits are bacteria, such as *Salmonella* and *Clostridium botulinum,* or toxins, such as aflatoxins (which derive from the bacteria *Aspergillus*) and vomitoxin (which is produced by *Fusarium* bacteria that grows in grain, especially wheat and barley). Vomitoxin affects dogs in particular. That toxin is the reason the FDA established a guideline that the grain and grain by-product composition of pet food should never exceed 40 percent.

Unless your dog cavorts through garbage cans and enjoys ingesting critters that were dead when he found them, he is unlikely to have food poisoning. Start avoiding problems with food safety by not allowing your pet to eat garbage or dead critters (not that you always have control over that). If you feed canned food, cover and refrigerate leftovers. Check dry food for mold; do not buy more than you can use in about a month, and store it in a cool, dry place. Clean food bowls often, not just by rinsing them out, but by washing in hot soapy water. Plastic food bowls can harbor more bacteria than metal or ceramic bowls do, so avoid the plastic bowls for anything but temporary use.

diets are considered prescription food and can be found at your veterinarian's clinic.

It can sometimes be difficult to ascertain if your dog has inhalant allergies or sarcoptic mange (caused by a type of mite) instead of food and/or other allergies. Your vet will want to know if your pet's itching is seasonal, if he's been treated unsuccessfully for sarcoptic mange, or if he has responded poorly to cortisone treatments for itching. Flea allergy is a common cause of severe itchiness, so make sure your dog is not suffering from fleas before switching his diet.

As with people, a dog can go on a food-elimination diet to see if he has a food allergy, and what is causing it. The dog will be given a hypoallergenic diet for a set period of time; if he stops itching, you go back to the original diet for up to two weeks to see if the itching returns. If your dog gets better with the test diet and starts itching again with the regular diet, then he has a food allergy. At that point, your dog can either go back to a hypoallergenic diet,

Puppies need more calories than adult dogs.

or you can try alternate protein diets. If the food-elimination diet doesn't change anything, then it's most likely that your dog has an inhalant allergy rather than a food allergy.

AGE-APPROPRIATE FEEDING

Puppies

It takes calories to grow, plus puppies burn a lot of calories by playing and rolling and romping. They require so many nutrients as puppies that it's almost double what adults need.

When you bring your puppy home, don't change his diet right away. Ask whoever you are getting the puppy from (a breeder of mixed dogs, rescue group, shelter, or the kind-hearted soul who found a litter by the side of the road) what the puppy has been eating, how much, and when. There's enough stress in going to a new home without adding preventable gastrointestinal distress. Use whatever food your puppy is used to for a few weeks, and keep the same schedule; then, if you want to change to something else, go ahead—slowly.

If you let puppies eat as much as they wish when they wish

by leaving a bowl of food available at all times, a practice called *free feeding*, you'll have a harder time with housetraining than you would if you fed on a schedule. Food follows a predictable path, and once you've established how long it takes after a meal before the puppy has to have a bowel movement, you can avoid middle-of-the-night mishaps.

While the puppy's eating schedule is obviously based on your daily schedule, feed a puppy under six months of age three or four times a day. Move to twice a day when your puppy is between six months and a year, and you can maintain that twice a day schedule throughout adulthood. After a meal, your puppy should nap for about an hour and a half to avoid getting an upset stomach.

A puppy needs more water than an adults dog does because water is part of that huge growth process. The state of growing creates wastes that get excreted in the blood. To remove those wastes from the blood, the dog needs to flush them through the kidneys with water and urinate them out. Let your puppy drink as much as he wants during the times you schedule him to drink so that he gets enough water.

Large- or Giant-Breed Puppies

What constitutes the best nutrition for puppies of large breeds is a bit controversial. If you think your mixed-breed puppy will be over 60 pounds (27 kg) or so as an adult, carefully consider the nutrition the puppy will receive during those critical developmental periods.

Portion Control

It's not valid to just say "use X amount of food at each meal for a dog who weighs X pounds." The quantity of kibble given partially depends on its quality; more filler and less meat means you need to give more kibble to make up the nutrition. This is partially why premium foods may seem more expensive but end up being a better deal in the long run.

Read the label to discern the appropriate portion size. That recommendation will most likely need to be adjusted to your dog's activity level, age, health, and weight. Just because he ate a full cup of Brand X twice a day three years ago doesn't mean he's going to need the same quantity of Brand Y. Activity level often goes hand in hand with age, but not always. One 75-pound (34-kg) dog may need more food than another 75-pound (34-kg) dog to keep the same weight. Experiment with quantity until you discover that your dog is not gaining or losing weight on a given quantity.

The same goes for any diet, including home-cooked or raw diets. In the beginning of a new diet, try weighing your dog more frequently to make sure he is not gaining or losing an inappropriate amount of weight; as bad as it is when a slightly overweight dog gains weight, it's far more frightening when a scrawny dog loses weight.

Physiologically speaking, rapid growth is not a good idea because it contributes to many medical problems, such as hip dysplasia (malformed hips, which can be a significant problem in big breeds even without rapid growth), hypertrophic osteodystrophy (inflammatory bone disease of rapidly growing puppies), and osteochondrosis (abnormality in developing cartilage). Rapid weight gain and a high-calorie diet in puppies apparently increase the severity of hip dysplasia.

Research the topic of feeding large-breed puppies, and then discuss your concerns and preferences with your veterinarian. Many vets believe large- and giant-breed puppies should be fed a normal commercial puppy ration without any supplements, as oversupplementation may contribute to the development of these painful orthopedic problems.

Commercial Raw Diets

Prepared raw pet food diets are available from some manufacturers. The food in these diets is usually organic, so they can be expensive, but the convenience is a big plus—someone else worries about proportions and providing a balanced diet. Some manufactures will ship the food, often frozen, directly to you.

Adults

Adults can be fed once or twice a day, but twice is much better and easier on their systems. A few years ago, most vets said it was okay to feed adult dogs once a day. However, most now prefer that dogs be fed twice a day. Not many people can go all day with only one meal, so why should we expect our dogs to? Besides, dogs don't view food just as nourishment—on the contrary, indulging in food is a reason for living. Most dogs live to eat, they don't eat to live, so double their pleasure. Another reason to feed twice a day is that it's easier to maintain weight control when your dog's metabolism runs evenly rather than spiking once a day.

Adult dogs require protein, fat, and carbohydrates for energy. How much your dog needs is individual, and much of it depends on activity level and general health. If your dog runs with you every morning, or competes in agility or lure coursing, he will need more protein, fat, and calories than a dog whose main exercise is going around the block on a leash. Younger dogs are more active than older ones; therefore, as your dog ages, he will need less calories on a daily basis.

Unlike puppyhood, it's necessary to adjust the amount of food your adult dog gets for his own needs. Watch his weight and adjust accordingly. Account for seasonal differences too; if you live in a snowy winter climate, your dog will need a few more calories on winter days than he will on summer days—but only a few. We're not talking about an extra meal here, just some extra treats.

If your dog is underweight, whether from a medical condition or from being a stray before arriving at the shelter where you adopted him, talk to your veterinarian about his specific nutritional needs. It's possible a supplement will help, or maybe just more calories per day will be fine until the dog reaches an appropriate weight. Find out from your vet what an appropriate weight would be for your mixed breed.

Pregnant or Nursing Bitches

Bitches who are pregnant or nursing puppies need more food. Being pregnant and nursing puppies burn a ton of calories, and nutrition is critical. Typically, by the last week of pregnancy, a bitch will need about three times her normal level of calories.

(Hopefully, to reduce the number of unwanted dogs, you will choose to spay or neuter your mixed-breed dog before she produces an unexpected litter. Sadly, there are not enough good homes to go around; sometimes even responsible breeders of popular purebreds don't have enough homes for each puppy.)

Seniors

Seniors can continue their adult schedule of eating twice a day, but it may be necessary at some point to switch them to three times a day. Sometimes, as seniors age, they get too hungry to make it from dinner to breakfast and end up burping up a little bit because they're hungry. If that happens, a biscuit before bed should help.

The opposite of puppies, seniors need less calories, protein, and fat. They also need a bit more fiber. Aged dogs lose a bit more of the necessary electrolytes, vitamins, and minerals through their kidneys because they don't absorb them as well as young dogs do. Your senior may need a food change, or maybe just a little less of what he's been getting; once again, it's an individual decision.

Senior food is an area in which you must read labels and understand them. The pet food manufacturers make food specifically for seniors; sometimes it's unnecessary or a bad choice, sometimes it's quite beneficial. Most of it depends on your dog's kidneys and whether or not kidney function has changed with age. If your dog's kidney function has lessened, or changed somehow, the kidneys function better on less protein; that's why most senior foods have less protein than adult maintenance foods.

Depending on your dog's specific needs, prescription foods for

Teething

Puppies start teething around three or four months of age. Baby teeth fall out and adult teeth grow in. Needless to say, a puppy's jaw hurts while this is happening, and chewing helps relieve the pain. This process is why people tend to lose things like shoes and books to puppies; your puppy is not trying to be destructive or clean out your library to his taste. It just feels better when he puts pressure on his sore jaw, and he can only get that pressure by chewing on something. Your puppy doesn't know what shoes cost, nor does he understand any difference between your old comfy slippers and your fancy new pair of shoes for New Year's Eve.

Don't worry if your puppy turns into a temporary finicky eater during teething—he will most likely grow out of it.

kidney problems are available. However, don't just up and switch to a kidney-care food without asking your vet about it first. There's no need to switch because your dog's age just hit double digits.

Dogs are remarkably like people in many ways, and some seniors get constipated. Senior foods tend to have a little more fiber for this reason. You can select a commercial food with a higher fiber level or add psyllium husks. Psyllium husks come in the form of powder, which makes feeding it to some dogs a bit dicey. Canned food is an obvious choice in which to serve the powdered psyllium husks, but canned food is high in calories for senior dogs; if your dog is overweight at all, canned food is not going to help his overall health. However, you can mix the husks in with nonfat yogurt or pureed vegetables.

If a dog who loves to eat loses interest in food, there are many potential causes for lack of interest. First, have your vet check your dog's teeth; it's hard to eat with dental pain, and dental pain is typically worse while eating. Dogs are always prone to gingivitis, but they can also get tooth abscesses, cavities, and loose teeth. Sometimes a smaller sized kibble will help keep your dog eating, or you can add water to soften his regular food. Seniors can't chew the way they did in their youth. If it's easier, switch to more meals per day with less food per meal.

Some senior dogs just aren't as interested in food as they used to be. There may not be a medical cause behind it, just a slowing down of the body. Sometimes dogs don't eat because they're sick; in that case, switching foods isn't going to do much good. Get your dog in for a physical examination if you notice any appetite changes.

Feed your adult mix twice a day.

Feeding Puppies

Puppies under 6 months of age should be fed three times per day, but puppies over 6 months but under 12 months should be fed twice a day.

NUTRITIONAL SUPPLEMENTS

Supplements are not necessary, or even appropriate, for healthy adult dogs. A basic vitamin pill can't hurt adults, but too much of

Poisonous Foods

Some foods that are fine for people are actually toxic, or poisonous, to dogs. While you shouldn't worry if your dog grabs a tiny piece of chocolate out of your hand, be aware of how much he's eaten.

Toxicity is based on dosage, weight, and sensitivity; that means that six birth control pills aren't going to have the same effect on a 108-pound (49-kg)) dog that they will on a 9-pound (4-kg) dog.

If your dog manages to eat more than just a tiny bit of one of the following foods, call your veterinarian or the fee-based ASPCA National Poison Control Center at (888) 426-4435.

Alcohol: Whether from beverages or cleaning agents, it can depress the central nervous system and cause a coma

Caffeine: A central nervous system stimulant that causes vomiting, diarrhea, hyperactivity

Chocolate: Can cause cardiovascular difficulties, central nervous system stimulation, vomiting, diarrhea, hyperactivity seizures; baker's chocolate is the worst

Garlic: Far less toxic than onions and often healthful in small quantities but a potential cause of red blood cell problems and hemolytic anemia when ingested in large quantities

Grapes/raisins: Large amounts can cause acute kidney failure

Macadamia nuts: Can cause movement difficulties and dogs can't get up

Moldy food: Can cause a range of problems from diarrhea to mycotoxin poisoning

Onions or onion powder: Onion toxicity develops into hemolytic anemia

Potatoes: Particularly dangerous when they turn green

Salt: Can cause pancreatitis or bloat

Xylitol: A canine-toxic sweetener found in products such as gum, mints, candy

Yeast dough: A dog's body heat causes the yeast dough in the stomach to expand, which can cause pain, bloat, and vomiting; dogs can require a surgical repair and treatment for alcohol toxicosis

specialized supplements can be cause for concern. However, your vet may recommend some supplements for the health of your mix.

Dogs with allergies can benefit from essential fatty acids in the form of omega-3 and omega-6 fatty acids, fish oil, flax seed oil, or vitamin E. The marketplace has many products, so pick and choose what might work best. Brewer's yeast, which boasts protein, zinc, and biotin, helps some dog with allergies; as with most supplements, brewer's yeast may not work for every dog, and some dogs don't do well on it. You may have to experiment with trial and error before you find a combination that works for your dog.

Senior dogs may need a vitamin and mineral pill. Seniors can benefit from antioxidants, which can slow down aging. Antioxidants neutralize harmful free radicals as well as help protect

Overweight dogs can suffer from many health problems; it's up to you to get your mix back on track!

the body's cells and tissues. Geriatric specialists often recommend antioxidants once a breakdown in body systems has begun. Once you've started your geriatric mixed breed on antioxidants, it's best to keep him on for life. Read the labels on the vitamins you wish to use to see if it lists antioxidants.

Glucosamine and chondroitin can be an incredible boon to arthritic dogs—they can truly make a difference in comfort level. These can help any bone or joint concern. Typically, these supplements are not used until dogs are seniors, but if your dog had a joint injury at a young age, these supplements may improve his quality of life before he becomes a senior.

Constipated dogs may need fiber. You can increase your adult dog's fiber intake by offering bran cereal, or mix powdered psyllium husks with canned food or plain yogurt. (Psyllium husks bought in bulk from a health food store are less expensive than those small containers you can buy at the drug store.) Ask your veterinarian for a specific dosage for your dog.

For dogs recuperating from such medical events as cancer or liver trouble, or dogs who have a chronic condition like diabetes, supplements can be a great idea. Supplements you buy at the vet clinic are of higher quality but cost more. If money is an issue, give the higher quality ones during major ill health, and the less expensive ones during and after recovery.

OBESITY

Obesity is the largest (no pun intended) nutritional problem among dogs; estimates of obesity in dogs range from about 25 percent to 40 percent of the dog population, at least in the United States. Obesity is defined being 10 to 25 percent above the dog's ideal weight. An ideal weight depends on your dog's body type, and with mixed breeds it can be a little harder for owners to figure out what an appropriate weight range is. Ask your vet about your mix's ideal weight.

Obesity contributes to many serious medical problems in dogs, just as it does in people. Obese dogs—those adorable little sausage-like guys who beg without shame or mercy—are prone to diabetes mellitus; orthopedic problems such as hip dysplasia, cruciate ligament ruptures, and herniated intervertebral disks; heart disease, including congestive heart failure; respiratory disease; kidney disease; liver disease; heat intolerance; potentially life-threatening pancreatitis; mammary tumors; and bladder cancer. They are also more likely to have strokes and heart attacks.

Other diseases are aggravated by obesity, including arthritis, epilepsy, tracheal collapse, and respiratory disease. These are uncomfortable conditions at the best of times, and adding extra weight into the diagnosis just makes it harder for them to feel good. Because fatty tissue is vascular, obese dogs are more likely to bleed during surgery, and anesthesia use is more complicated. Obesity increases heat and exercise intolerance, meaning an obese dog can get into a cycle that doesn't end: He can't exercise because of the heat, and he can't lose weight because of the lack of exercise.

Kibble Lite

"Lite" kibbles are available for overweight dogs, but hopefully if you cut back on treats and increase exercise, you won't have to resort to that.

Obese dogs may have weakened immune systems as a direct result of their weight. They are more likely to have skin problems than dogs of a healthy weight, and skin problems are already the main reason people bring their dog to the vet, even without the complication of obesity. Being overweight complicates the use of drugs because of the changed metabolism. An obese dog recovers from injuries more slowly than does a dog of appropriate weight.

An overweight dog doesn't live as long as a lean one. To help your dog live longer, and be around for years, keep his weight and exercise level to appropriate proportions.

How Can I Tell If My Mix Is Overweight?

A rib check is the fastest way to check if your dog is overweight. Simply put, if you can't feel your dog's ribs, he's overweight. Of course, it's not quite that simple, but it's a quick and obvious guide. Veterinarians use a 9-point scoring system for body condition. A score of 9 means the dog is morbidly obese. A score of 4.5 is just where your dog should be. A score of 1 is usually only seen in starving strays.

Feel your dog's ribs. You should be able to feel them easily. While there should be a tiny bit of protective fat covering the rib cage, you should be aware of each individual rib. If you can't, it's time for less fuel and more exercise. Look at your dog from above: Dogs should have a waistline behind their ribs (although this is harder to see in a long-coated mixed breed). If you can't see a waistline, he's overweight. If you look from the side, he should

If your mix is overweight, it's time to review his feeding habits.

have an *abdominal tuck*—the area behind your dog's ribs should be smaller than his chest.

Medical Causes

In dogs, certain thyroid conditions contribute to obesity. It is possible that your dog's weight has little bearing on how much he eats, but thyroid trouble isn't nearly as common as sheer overeating. Have your vet check your dog's thyroid with a simple blood test. If there is a thyroid problem, the inexpensive medication must be taken daily for the rest of the dog's life. If the thyroid tests are normal, there are no other physical problems, and your dog is still too heavy, increase his level of exercise and lower his food intake.

Weight Watchers

It's a sad fact of life for most people and dogs that, as we age and become a little fonder of relaxing on the couch watching television and eating snacks, we gain weight at a faster rate than we did in our active, more highly metabolic youth. Less calories are needed to maintain the same weight. This fact has nothing to do with a specific breed, and tiny mixes and Mastiff mixes can gain weight just as fast as those sausage-like Lab mixes we see waddling into the vet's office. It's the same the world over and across all species: Too much fuel translates into weight gain.

If your mixed breed—tiny or humongous—is too fat to enjoy a nice walk after dinner, that beloved dog stands a good chance of having a shorter lifespan than he would if he weren't overweight. Since you are in charge of the food regulation, despite your dog's attempted forays into the garbage, you can help him lose weight.

Start by cutting out treats and table scraps. That's where the real problem usually comes from anyway, so if you just don't give those anymore, that's half the battle. The calories in treats add up quickly. If you are going to dog school classes, incorporate the calories in training treats into the daily allotment. At home, try giving toys instead of treats so that your dog will burn calories instead of

Chewing

It may sound odd, but chewing can take up too much training time. A hard treat can break concentration while your dog chomps down, so soft treats are best for training.

taking them in. Many dogs like green beans or carrots, and for those dogs, these vegetables make healthy treats.

Also, keep an eye on children. They love to give dogs treats and may be giving your dog more than you think he's getting. If your dog needs to shed some weight, have the children give him carrots or bite-sized pieces of apple. Like children, dogs have no idea of what is good for them, and it's up to us to keep them from being their own worst enemies.

Increasing your dog's exercise makes a big difference. Unlike a lot of people, dogs love to go for walks and get some exercise. They tend to become couch potatoes if their people are couch potatoes; the more you walk, the more they walk. Exercise also brings a bit of socialization, so it's a win-win situation.

Since you are in control of what your dog eats, it is up to you to ensure his health by keeping him at an appropriate weight. The amounts of food suggested by pet food manufacturers assume that the dog is getting regular exercise; if you and your dog are happy being couch potatoes, your dog will need less food than is stated on the label.

Of course, if you don't let your dog get fat in the first place, you won't have to reduce his daily allotment. If you feed to maintain an ideal body condition throughout your mixed breed's lifespan, you may contribute greatly to your pet's longevity.

Calorie Counting

Do not use treats as meals. Remember, they are *treats*; account for them in your dog's daily caloric intake.

TREATS

No matter how much Chihuahua or yellow Lab is in your mixed breed, or how much he weighs, eating too many treats can cause weight gain. Be particularly careful with tiny dogs because it doesn't take much for them to gain weight; after all, if 1 pound (0.5 kg) is 15 percent of your dog's body weight, it only takes one extra pound for him to become overweight.

When your dog is a puppy, treats don't seem too harmful. After all, puppies have high metabolisms and, because they play from sun up to sun down, they burn calories all day long. But as your dog becomes an adult, the calories in those treats can add up rapidly. Since your dog wouldn't count calories even if he could, it's up to you to count the calories for him.

Some dog treats are junk food, while some are good for a dog. Dried liver and rawhide are two very different types of treats. Sure, rawhide takes a long time for your dog to chew through and will

Make sure that the treats you give your mix are healthy.

keep him occupied, but it has a lot of calories and fat. Plus, your dog can get pancreatitis from too many rawhides. Dried liver is the more nutritious option.

Those popular green dental chews are also fairly high in calories. They can help out with dog breath, but some dogs have a bad digestive reaction to them and end up vomiting little green piles. Supervise your dog while he's enjoying a chewable manufactured bone because those treats can cause choking or create a bowel blockage known as a *foreign obstruction*. (Pantyhose and rocks also create foreign obstructions, but hopefully you're not giving those as treats.)

Training Treats

Training can be a joy with your mixed breed, and most dogs prefer food rewards to anything else (food proffered with a kiss is often best). Training treats are terrific motivators, particularly if they consist of foods that your dog doesn't get outside of training.

Food-motivated dogs—and you know what they're like if you share your home with one —are easy to train using food as a positive reinforcer. It's a bit like your boss holding ice cream or a pan of lasagna over your head if you get that messed-up spreadsheet fixed before the meeting starts. It's wise to use treats during training, but take care to calculate the calories into the dog's total daily intake.

Break up treats into small pieces so that you can pass out more treats without overdoing the calorie load. It helps to switch the treats around so that there is something new and stinky (*treat du jour*) that will help motivate your dog. Even if your dog would turn somersaults for freeze-dried liver on Tuesday, by Saturday he may think that a peanut butter dog cookie is the best substance on the planet (other than canned food, which is incredibly hard to use as a training treat).

Use nutritious treats such as low-fat cheese or tiny pieces of hot dogs as opposed to treats that are just empty calories, even though your dog probably would set a long jump world record for something that would give him really bad diarrhea. The need for good nutrition never stops.

TABLE MANNERS

I know an owner who has a sign in her kitchen: "Cook is not responsible for dog hair in the food." While most dog lovers easily understand this, we forget that some people who may not care for dogs will visit your house. For these folks in particular, you want your dog to be polite while dinner is on the table. Even dog people like to eat without being molested by begging, whining, drooling dogs.

Good table manners for dogs mean:
- Dogs should not beg at the table.
- Dogs should not be get table scraps while at the table.
- Dogs should not paw someone's knee to beg.
- Dogs should not jump on a kitchen chair to stare at someone while they eat.
- Dogs should not bark to notify you that there is a bit of pizza crust that you obviously don't want because there it is on the table.

You may think those big brown manipulative eyes begging for food is cute, but not everyone does. Besides, if you let your dog beg and eat table scraps while you're sitting at the table, even after the coffee is made, you are paving the way for excessive calorie consumption. Your guests will have every right to be upset if a dog tongue curls onto their plate, or they spend the entire meal with a dog breathing heavily on their ankles. This behavior is not cute, even if you think it is.

Dogs should eat their meals in their own bowls at their assigned place, even on Thanksgiving when there are 14 guests dropping crumbs on the living room carpeting. Keep your dog's meal routine even when you are serving nonroutine meals to other people.

Resist that pleading look— begging only leads to bad manners!

Chapter

5

GROOMING

Your Mixed Breed

For mixed breeds, grooming needs can be all over the map. Some dogs require no grooming other than an occasional brushing, and some need so much grooming that the services of a professional groomer should be used. So how do you know what's best for your mixed breed, especially if you don't know what breeds he's mixed with?

The bottom line is fairly simple: Dogs who have hair, not fur, do not shed. (Well, they do shed a tiny bit, but nothing noticeable.) Dogs with hair, like Poodle mixes, need haircuts. You can do it yourself or take the dog to a professional groomer, depending on your skill, confidence, and financial position. Dogs with fur, like Husky mixes, shed and do not need haircuts. They need brushing.

There is nothing any dog likes so much as individual, full attention from you—it contributes to his sense of feeling loved.

GROOMING AS HEALTH CARE

Grooming serves two purposes. It improves a dog's appearance, but it's also an effective form of preventive health care. For dogs, the majority of veterinary visits are related to skin problems. The status of a dog's skin speaks volumes about his general health and nutrition.

So, while you are brushing your dog (which is necessary for dogs with fur and those with hair) take the opportunity to check on the status of his skin. Look for lumps, fleas, mites, hair mats, cuts, bites, runny eyes, and anything else that you notice as being a bit out of the normal range for your dog. Don't forget that as he ages, he will get a few more bumps and lumps all over his skin; you want to keep an eye on them in case there's a chance that one of those lumps might not be harmless. The sooner you discover any problem, the easier it will be to treat. In this respect, a dog with a short coat is easier to care for than a dog with a long coat.

Smooth-Coated Breeds

Your mixed-breed dog may have a smooth coat if he is a mix of one of these breeds:

- American Foxhound
- American Staffordshire Terrier
- Anatolian Shepherd
- Basenji
- Basset Hound
- Beagle
- Black and Tan Coonhound
- Bloodhound
- Boston Terrier
- Boxer
- Bulldog
- Bullmastiff
- Bull Terrier
- Chihuahua (smooth)
- Chinese Sharpei
- Chinese Crested
- Dalmatian
- Dachshund (smooth)
- Doberman Pinscher
- English Foxhound
- Fox Terrier (smooth)
- French Bulldog
- German Shorthaired Pointer
- Great Dane
- Greater Swiss Mountain Dog
- Greyhound
- Harrier
- Ibizan Hound
- Italian Greyhound
- Labrador Retriever
- Manchester Terrier (toy and standard)
- Mastiff
- Miniature Pinscher
- Parson/Jack Russell Terrier (smooth)
- Pharaoh Hound
- Pug
- Rhodesian Ridgeback
- Rottweiler
- Staffordshire Bull Terrier
- Toy Fox Terrier
- Vizsla
- Weimaraner
- Whippet

GROOMING EQUIPMENT

All dogs require certain basic grooming equipment, including a brush, flea comb, doggy toothbrush, doggy toothpaste, nail clipper, doggy shampoo, towels, scissors, cotton balls to clean ears, and an appropriate place in which to bathe the dog.

It's not necessary to have a grooming table unless you find the height of it is easier on your back or if your dog moves around so much that you really need the help of the neck noose to keep him from running off in the midst of your clipping and scissoring. A rubber bath mat on the kitchen counter will be fine. If you're going to use a clipper, make sure that the spot you've chosen is near an electrical outlet.

COAT TYPES

Your mixed breed's coat depends totally on heritage. And

although heritage creates the coat, it doesn't matter where it came from as long as you know how to approach it.

A short coat is less than 1 inch (2.5 cm) long. Long coats are typically found on dogs with hair that must be cut. Wirehaired, curly, and smooth (those that lie close to the skin) coats are somewhat different from either short or long coats. Short and smooth coats are the easiest to take care of and generally do not require professional grooming. Longhaired coats generally take the most time to groom.

Short Coats

For dogs with short coats, such as a Dalmatian/Basset Hound mix, brush in the direction that the coat grows about once a week.

Brushing

A curry brush (a thick plastic nibbed "brush" the size of your hand) works great for really smooth coats. Short coats also can be kept up with a *hound glove*, which is a glove with nibs on it that brush your dog's coat as you pet him. If you prefer a regular-type brush, short coats can take a stiff natural-bristle brush or a soft slicker brush, which has little bent metal pins in it.

Bathing

The frequency of bathing depends on the dog. Some dogs with short coats rarely need bathing, but others, such as Hound mixes, tend to have an oilier coat and need baths more often. Today's pet shampoos can't hurt, so you can bathe as often as you feel that your dog needs it.

This mix's short coat is easy to care for.

Drying the Coat

Towel dry this type of coat, or let it air dry.

Long Coats

For dogs with long coats that do not shed, such as a Bichon/Chow Chow mix, brush every day. Regular brushing helps to remove loose hair and keep it from matting; skin mats can be irritating to your dog, so brushing is not just a matter of appearance. A flea comb helps to get rid of small tidbits, like fleas, flea dirt, and bits of debris that dogs pick up like magnets.

If you don't physically cut this long coat, it will continue to grow so long that the dog will step on it, causing a locomotion problem. It's just like your hair—it doesn't stop growing at a given point like the hair of short-coated dogs. Also, if you don't brush the long coat regularly, it can mat and tangle, and cause some skin irritations. To avoid the mats and tangles, brush daily.

For dogs with long coats that shed, such as Golden Retriever/ Irish Setter mixes, daily brushing isn't necessary, but it still should be done several times a week as needed. Unfortunately, if brushing isn't done regularly, large knotty mats will form, particularly behind the ears and in the armpits, which will take patience to remove. It's much easier to brush regularly and frequently than to get rid of mats.

Brushing

A pin brush has short, straight metal pins that help you brush down to the skin and avoid the dreaded mats. Start close to the skin and brush away from it. If the long hair is already matted, use a comb to tease it out.

Bathing

Both veterinarians and groomers now agree that you can bathe a dog as often as necessary without worrying about the effect on the skin. How fast a dog's coat gets dirty depends both on his coat and on his behavior. (Many dogs like to roll in mud or the compost pile immediately after a bath or leap into muddy puddles during walks.) When you notice that your long-coated dog seems dirty, bathe him. You also can bathe on a regular schedule, such as once a month, depending on how fast your dog's coat gets dirty.

This mix's longer coat takes some time and effort to groom.

Drying the Coat

You can towel dry the long coat, but a blow dryer designed for dogs is helpful. First towel dry your dog, and then use the blow dryer as you brush his hair. Use a blow dryer designed for dogs rather than for people, because dogs don't tolerate heat as well as humans do.

Styling the Coat

Some dogs with long hair must have it styled. This applies mostly to mixes of breeds such as Maltese, Bichons, and Yorkies. Because your mix isn't going to be a show dog who must conform to a certain standard, go ahead and style his hair the way you want. You can leave it long and part the hair all the way from nose to tail so that it falls evenly on both sides of his body, a nice and easy style. If your dog has bangs, you can keep short bangs or tie up longer ones. Many people opt for the simple and cute puppy cut, which means that the hair is cut short, to pretty much the same length over the whole body, as it was when the dog was a puppy. That's an easy style to keep without much work. But if you like styling, you have many options.

This Peke-a-Poo mix has retained the Poodle's curly coat.

Curly Coats

Curly coats are usually seen in Maltipoos, Cockapoos, and any other Poodle mix. Many people who have curly-coated dogs choose to use a professional groomer because this coat grows continuously, and it can be hard for the average person to manage.

Because curly hair essentially stands away from the body, it's easy to scissor this coat or to use a clipper.

Brushing

A slicker brush is the best choice, followed by a once-over with a metal comb.

Bathing

These dogs need to be bathed a bit more often than other dogs because natural oils and dirt noticeably weigh down a curly coat.

Dealing With Mats

One unique problem encountered by dogs with long coats is that in certain areas that rub together, like armpits, behind the ears, and under the collar, the long hair can get badly matted. Pay plenty of attention to these problem areas before they get out of hand. As with other mats, tease them out. The trick here is to stay on top of those areas and prevent the mats from occurring in the first place.

If your mix has a wirehaired coat, it may need to be "stripped" occasionally.

Drying the Coat

If you are not using a groomer, blow dry your dog rather than towel dry, so that the curls are straightened out a bit for scissoring or cutting.

Wirehaired Coats

Thankfully, the wirehaired coat doesn't mat, or at least it doesn't mat much. The wiry characteristic of the coat keeps it from matting, so don't cut it short if you want it to resist matting. If you do cut the wiry coat of your Italian Spinone/German Wirehaired Pointer mix, you'll end up seeing mats as you do on any other longhaired dog.

Brushing

Brush a wirehaired coat about once a week. Use a slicker brush for the undercoat, if your dog has one. Comb afterward. A stripping knife will remove the dead hair in the undercoat.

Bathing

One nice feature of this coat is that you shouldn't bathe a wirehaired dog until he's really dirty. Bathing softens the coat, and the softness lessens the hair's ability not to mat. Brushing alone helps to keep the coat clean.

Drying the Coat

Air dry a dog with a wirehaired coat rather than toweling or blow drying.

Stripping the Coat

Depending on your mixed breed's wirehaired coat, it may be beneficial to pull out, by hand, the longest dead hairs. Use your finger and thumb to pull dead hairs from the overcoat so that the new coat grows continuously. Because it's labor intensive, it's expensive to have your groomer do it, and it's easy to do at home a bit at a time while you watch television or sit around the living room chatting. No tools are needed, although using a stripping knife or a contour file is easier on your hand.

BRUSHING

Not only does brushing remove loose or dead hair, but it also feels good to your pet.

Types of Brushes

What type of brush works best depends on your mixed breed's coat:

- **Slicker Brush:** A slicker brush is used for dogs with a wiry topcoat and a soft undercoat, as many terrier mixes have. Slicker brushes also should be used on dogs with short coats, such as Lab mixes, and dogs with wiry coats, such as Pointer mixes.
- **Wire Brush or Bristle Brush:** Dogs with long coats should have either a wire brush with long steel wires or a bristle brush. For dogs who have both an undercoat and a long coat, as would happen with a Northern breed mix, use the same wire or bristle brush.
- **Pin Brush:** Long but silky coats, such as Yorkie or Maltese

Long-Coated Breeds

Your mixed-breed dog may have a long coat if he is a mix of one of these breeds:

Afghan Hound	Dachshund (longhaired)	Lhasa Apso	Saint Bernard (longhaired)
Bearded Collie	English Cocker Spaniel	Löwchen	Samoyed
Briard	English Setter	Maltese	Shetland Sheepdog
Chihuahua (longhaired)	English Toy Spaniel	Newfoundland	Shih Tzu
Chinese Crested (powderpuff)	Gordon Setter	Old English Sheepdog	Silky Terrier
Cocker Spaniel	Havanese	Papillon	Skye Terrier
Chow Chow	Irish Setter	Pekingese	Tibetan Terrier
Collie (rough)	Japanese Chin	Polish Lowland Sheepdog	Yorkshire Terrier
	Keeshond	Pomeranian	

Find the right grooming equipment for your mix's coat type.

mixes, do well with pin brushes, as do the curlier coats that are seen in some Poodle mixes.

• **Rubber Brush or Hound Glove:** For some smooth coats, such as a Boxer or Pug mix, a rubber brush or hound glove work best. You just put the glove on and rub your hand over your dog, who thinks he's getting petted instead of brushed.

Dogs with long coats, such as those mixed with Golden Retriever, Irish Setter, English Setter, and spaniels, tend to have feathering. Feathering is the long loose hair that sometimes grows on the back legs. The longer a dog's feathering, the more he will benefit from regular brushing. Without brushing, long coats can mat, resulting in an unhappy dog with skin irritation.

How to Brush

Dogs should be brushed in the direction of hair growth. Start at the top of the head and brush toward the tail. Then go down the legs. Brush the chest and belly from the chest downward.

To remove a mat, either cut it with scissors, which sometimes does not leave a neat look, or buy either a slicker brush or a grooming tool specifically designed to remove mats. Also, it is sometimes possible to work mats out by pulling small amounts at a time from the side of each mat; some dogs have more patience for this than others.

BATHING

Oddly enough, many water-oriented dogs do not like baths. Neither do their purebred brethren. As a matter of fact, the vast majority of pet dogs feel that baths are either punishment or a form of water torture. It's your job to make bathing as easy as possible for your pet.

Types of Shampoo

There are so many kinds of shampoos available that selecting one can give you a headache. Just don't use your shampoo, because the pH balance for people is quite different than it is for dogs. Buy a shampoo especially formulated for dogs.

There are puppy shampoos designed for their delicate skin, hypoallergenic shampoos for dogs with allergies, whitening shampoos for white coats, tea tree and oatmeal shampoos for dogs with allergies, medicated shampoos for certain conditions such as seborrhea or fleas, deodorizing shampoos, shampoos mixed with moisturizers or hair conditioners, and so on.

One thing to remember is that, while you can use your cat's shampoo on your dog, it's best if you don't use your dog's shampoo on your cat. Cats have neurotoxic systems that are very different from dogs, and it's easy to unintentionally harm them by using products labeled for dogs.

How to Bathe

First, get all your supplies in one place. Then, place cotton balls in your dog's ears to prevent water from getting in and possibly irritating the eardrum.

Bathing is pretty much the same no matter what type of dog you have. After brushing the coat, insert your likely displeased dog into warm water (not hot—hot water will scald a dog's skin), add shampoo, scrub, rinse very thoroughly several times, and get the dog out of the water. Don't make the mistake of just shampooing his back; make sure that you get his belly, under his legs, around his groin, and his face. When you clean around his face, go slowly so that you don't get shampoo in his eyes.

In nice weather, your dog can

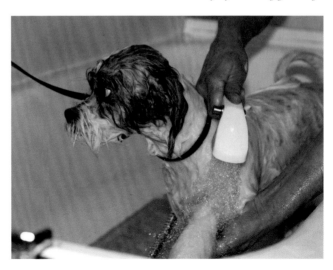

A handheld sprayer is useful for bathing your dog.

dry outside, although when he goes outside when wet, he will pick up more dirt and debris from the yard. However, he will probably be a lot happier if left to his own devices in the backyard than if he has to stay inside after the unpleasantness of a bath. In winter weather, or if you don't have a safe backyard, your dog can either dry naturally or you can use a dog-specific hair dryer (human hair dryers are too hot for canine skin). Whether you use a dryer or not, be sure to towel dry your dog before he leaves the bathing area.

How often you bathe your dog depends on several factors. For most dogs, once a month is enough, but some dogs, like Basenji mixes, are cat-like in their cleanliness and rarely, if ever, need baths. Double-coated breeds only need a few baths a year—if that—because their coats are essentially insulated and waterproofed by nature. If you wash too often, the coat and skin can become dry. Of course, your bathing schedule may go out the window if your dog rolls in something delightfully stinky. If, for some reason, this happens twice in one week, say once with fish and once with a long-dead rodent, you may want to bathe twice that week. In that case, use a hypoallergenic shampoo because they are designed not to dry out the skin.

CUTTING THE COAT

Have a towel ready to dry off your mix after his bath.

Mixed breeds who will most likely need to have their coats cut by either clipping or scissoring include Poodles, terriers, toy breeds, and any dog referred to as "hypoallergenic." What dog people mean by hypoallergenic is that the dog does not shed because he has hair that grows, just like human hair. With mixes of only one breed that doesn't shed, genetics will determine what the coat is like, so Poodle/Basset Hound mixes who get Poodle coats will need clipping, and Poodle/Basset Hound mixes who get Basset coats will not.

Clipping

You can learn to use an electric clipper, save tons of money, and bond with your dog at the same time. Do not be intimidated by the thought of learning to use a clipper on your nonshedding dog. It's not as if your mixed-breed dog will be shown in conformation anyway, so just go for it. There are several good products on the market as well as instructional videos for those who find it easier to watch it being done than to grasp it from illustrations in books.

Don't cut yourself off at the knees by using a cheap clipper. Get a nice mid-range one rated for professional or show dog use; those cheap ones marketed for "pet use" fall apart pretty quickly. Also, the nicer ones handle much better, and you will be more easily convinced that you can do this. For the price of two grooming sessions, you can buy a nice clipper that will last several years. Go into a pet store and play around with the display models to see which one you prefer. Some people like the cordless variety because it's easier not to have the cord in the way, but they are less powerful than the corded ones.

How to Clip

Before you clip, brush out mats, or if you're desperate, cut them out.

Start clipping your mixed breed on the face; if your dog has a beard, start there. Then do the sides of the face, between the eyes, and then the top of the head and down the body. Next, clip the legs. Use scissors for the face, around the ears, and the tail. Be careful around your dog's anus, because if you hurt that sensitive area, he might always have a rather justified dislike of the clipper.

Should You Learn to Use a Clipper?

In the beginning of your clipping "career," your dog will not look like he does after the professional groomer takes care of him.

Only you can decide if the cost of professional grooming on a regular basis is worth it to you. You can get good at clipping if you try; however, if the idea makes you feel itchy all over, don't attempt it. You don't want to have a bad experience coming in between you and your dog. You also could explore a combination of sessions, such as professional grooming every other session, with you clipping at home in the meantime. The longer you go between sessions, and the longer the hair gets, the harder it will be to clip your dog.

You can watch all the grooming videos in the world, but what can only be learned by experience is how much pressure you need to remove a given amount of hair. Too much pressure will cut the coat too short, and insufficient pressure won't make enough difference. The hard part in the learning process is that you can't try it every day until you get a really good handle on it; you only can clip your dog every six weeks or so. But you can get the hang of it, enjoy the financial savings, and relish in the bonding that occurs when you and your dog do something together.

Wirehaired/Broken-Coated Breeds

Your mixed-breed dog may have a wirehaired/broken coat if he is a mix of one of these breeds:

Affenpinscher

Airedale Terrier

Australian Terrier

Border Terrier

Bouvier des Flandres

Brussels Griffon

Cairn Terrier

Dachshund (wirehaired)

Dandie Dinmont Terrier

Fox Terrier (wire)

German Wirehaired Pointer

Schnauzer: Giant, Standard, and Miniature

Irish Terrier

Irish Wolfhound

Parson and Jack Russell Terriers (wirehaired)

Lakeland Terrier

Norfolk Terrier

Norwich Terrier

Otterhound

Petit Basset Griffon Vendeen

Scottish Deerhound

Scottish Terrier

Sealyham Terrier

Soft Coated Wheaten Terrier

Welsh Terrier

West Highland White Terrier

Wirehaired Pointing Griffon

Sadly, just as with toenails, if you clip the thin papery skin around the ears, it will bleed a lot. Apply pressure and use styptic power or flour to stop the bleeding.

Oil the clipper's moving parts three times, before you start, somewhere about halfway through the process, and again at the end after you're through clipping and before you put the clipper away for storage.

Scissoring

Considered a high-ticket service at the groomer's because of the amount of labor involved, you also can just scissor your dog by hand instead of using a clipper. Understand that urgent vet calls are not made because of clippers, although many dogs are seen on an urgent basis for a scissors cut. Use caution!

How to Scissor

Use a good pair of sharp grooming scissors; choose anything less and you'll be ripping your own hair out. It's all too easy to accidentally cut a dog with scissors, even for experienced folks, so use caution when you decide to take scissors in hand. Squirmy dogs may have their own ideas about the suitability of scissors by their eyes and privates. For the body, select regular grooming scissors, and use them on larger areas such as the back and chest.

Cut down the back and down the legs. Use smaller, shorter grooming scissors with rounded tips rather than pointed ones for the ears, head, face, and groin areas.

Curly coats are incredibly forgiving of scissoring mistakes, and even a novice can't go wrong with scissoring a curly coat. The straighter the hair, the more visible your inexperience will be. But you'll only be inexperienced for a relatively short time, and then you'll be on your way to enjoying scissoring, if not on your way to grooming school.

NAIL TRIMMING

Most dogs like nail trimming even less than baths, if that's imaginable. Sure, there's always a dog here and there who hands you his paw and says with impunity, "Okay, Mom, chop 'em off," but the reality is that many dogs dislike having their nails trimmed.

Dog experts recommend that you touch a puppy's toes and nails frequently when he's little just to get him used to it for toenail trimming. However, many mixed breeds arrive at their forever homes from the shelter, well past puppyhood, in which case their feelings about toenail trimming are usually set in stone. However, the sooner you teach a puppy or an adult to accept it, the easier it will be for you for the rest of your dog's life.

Use a sharp trimmer, which will make the "procedure" quicker, and replace it every few years.

How to Trim the Nails

If you can hear your dog's nails on the floor as he walks by, they're too long and need to be trimmed. Some dogs don't mind nail trimming, while others prefer to avoid it like the plague. If you feel that you cannot trim the nails yourself, ask your veterinarian or groomer to trim them.

Use a clipper designed to trim dog nails. Just take the nail clipper in hand, hold the paw, and use your fingers to separate one toe from the rest. You only want to clip the hook-like part that turns downward.

In a dog's nail, the *quick* is where the vein that feeds the nail ends and the dry dead nail to be trimmed begins. If you trim the quick, it bleeds. The idea is to cut below the quick and just trim dead nail, because toes

Quick Tip

If you brush your dog's coat again before it dries, it is less likely to mat.

Be careful not to cut the quick when clipping your dog's nails.

107

are heavy bleeders, and some dogs find cutting the quick to be uncomfortable or painful. It's especially hard to see the quick on black toenails; the quick is visible as a pink or red line within white toenails. However, everybody cuts a quick once in a while. The more often you trim the nail, the less likely that is to happen.

If you do cut the quick, and your dog is waving a bleeding nail at you, put a clean towel or tissue on the nail and apply pressure for five to ten minutes until the bleeding stops. Styptic powder and gels can shorten the length of time that the nail bleeds.

EAR CARE

The longer the ears, the more likely it is that your dog will have ear infections. Yeast and bacteria love the moist climate in ears. In fact, dog ears are one of nature's best bacteria catchers, and they are a perfect place for yeast to grow, particularly for mixes of breeds with very long ears such as Cocker Spaniels and Basset Hounds. Most ear infections are a relatively minor (albeit possibly chronic and definitely irritating) infection that is usually responsive to antibiotic ointments and cleansing flushes. Look for redness and swelling inside the ear.

If your mixed breed has cute, perky prick ears, that doesn't mean that he won't get any ear infections. Any dog can get ear infections.

Check your dog's ears for foreign bodies.

How to Care for Your Dog's Ears

Prevention makes a huge, positive difference. Before a bath, flush out your dog's ears with commercial cleaning preparations found at the vet's. Do this before a bath because the cleansers can dirty his coat and make it a bit sticky in some cases.

Squeeze a few drops of the ear-cleaning solution into the ear and then gently rub the outside of both sides of the ear canal to make sure that the solution goes in deeply. Most dogs will shake their heads to get rid of the solution, but they won't get rid of all of it because of how deeply you placed it. It is a good idea to take a step back so that you don't get the solution on your clothes. After

Curly-Coated Breeds

Your mixed-breed dog may have a curly coat if he is a mix of one of these breeds:

American Water Spaniel

Bedlington Terrier

Bichon Frise

Curly-Coated Retriever

Irish Water Spaniel

Kerry Blue Terrier

Komondor

Poodle: Standard, Miniature, and Toy

Portuguese Water Dog

Puli

flushing, rinse the hair or fur affected at the bottom of the ear. Keep the ears dry and clean during a bath by popping in a cotton ball. (Never use cotton swabs to clean out your dog's ears; they can damage the ear canal, and swabs simply shove all the wax into the canal, which can harm the ear.)

Foreign bodies, such as grass or weed seeds, can get stuck in the ear and cause an infection. Grooming is an excellent time to search for these foes. Some of these foreign objects, like foxtails, are painful enough that your veterinarian will need anesthesia to examine or clean the ear. Some of these incidents may require medication. At any rate, regularly flushing ears before baths can help to ward off ear infections.

EYE CARE

Some dogs get a lot of mucus built up in their eyes. Sometimes that mucus dries up in the interior corner of the dog's eye into a hard kind of crusty goo.

How to Care for Your Dog's Eyes

Use a tissue, cotton ball, or your fingers to gently remove any eye discharge. If the discharge seems excessive, have your vet look at it. The inner eyelids should not be swollen or have a yellow discharge.

If your dog is having eye problems, he may have a lot of discharge both from the disease and from the ointments and drops used to treat it. The buildup of this dry discharge can cause a large mat. Run warm water onto a washcloth, and slowly work away at the dried buildup. Otherwise, a very irritating mat can form in a

The Nylon Coat

To keep dog hair from sticking to you, purchase a nylon coat for yourself at a dog show or pet supply store. Unlike polar fleece, which attracts dog hair like a magnet, clipped-off dog hair does not get all over a nylon coat. You may think that these grooming coats are a waste of money until you realize that you don't have to wash your clothes each time you use a clipper. If you're going to get serious about clipping, consider a grooming coat for your own sake.

place where there is already a lot of irritation.

Hair that hangs into a dog's eyes can irritate and even scratch the surface of the cornea. Take care, then, to avoid letting hair contact the eye.

DENTAL CARE

Brushing your dog's teeth is as important, if not more important, than brushing his coat. If you neglect this aspect of his care, periodontal disease could result, a condition caused by the buildup of plaque and tartar. Therefore, you need to remove plaque and tartar every day. The rotten part is that if you don't, harmful bacteria could spread from his mouth to his bloodstream and then spread to other organs such as the kidneys, liver, and heart. That's why dental care is so critical to your dog's overall health.

Veterinarians recommend that you brush your dog's teeth daily.

How to Care for Your Dog's Teeth

To brush your dog's teeth, use a pet toothbrush and pet toothpaste. Human toothpaste is not supposed to be swallowed (not even by people) because of the detergents in it. And, because it's impossible to get a dog to gargle or rinse, pet toothpastes are designed to be swallowed. They come in a variety of fun doggy flavors, including poultry, liver, and peanut butter. (Most dogs don't particularly enjoy mint.) You also can buy toothpastes at the vet that have enzymes to help get rid of plaque.

You can use a finger brush to clean your dog's teeth.

Using a soft-bristled toothbrush, hold the brush so that the bristles are at a 45-degree angle. Position the brush between the gums and the back teeth in the mouth. Gently brush between the back area and then slowly move forward to the teeth in the front. Try to get the bristles around the base of a tooth and between teeth. Use short back-and-forth movements. Switch and do the other side. Pay most attention to the outer side of the teeth and the back teeth, because that's where plaque and tartar accumulate most. Dogs don't get nearly as much tartar buildup on the inside surfaces of their teeth (adjacent to the tongue), so consider the outside surfaces the priority. Your vet also can demonstrate how to brush your dog's teeth.

I'm Ready for My Closeup, Mr. DeMille

You may have gone to a dog show and seen dogs being groomed who look like they're on a beach enjoying 'brelly drinks. Do not assume that your mixed breed is going to hang out on a grooming table like a lounge lizard basking in the sun just because you've spent money on the clipper and table. Those show dogs you saw were not born knowing to stand calmly while electric clippers whoosh all over and hair spray is used in their nether regions. They had to learn to accept all facets of grooming, and so will your dog.

If your dog is a puppy when he joins your family, introduce him slowly to the different pieces of equipment. Don't try to use every piece of grooming equipment that you bought in a half hour. Neither of you are going to enjoy it or forget it. Have one short session for each piece of equipment.

Approach a new-to-you adult dog as slowly as you would a puppy until you know how he reacts to the equipment. It's possible that whoever had him before didn't groom him well or didn't bother with grooming at all. His previous owner may have hurt his skin so much that he now fears grooming.

However long it takes for your dog to accept grooming, you can do it! Ralph Waldo Emerson said, "Nothing great was achieved without enthusiasm," and this applies to your dog learning to accept something that he feels is unnatural.

Most dogs should have an annual dental cleaning under anesthesia. Afterward, you'll be surprised by how wonderfully white your pet's teeth are and how much better his "dog breath" smells. Today, the health risks from periodontal disease are more significant than the low risk from anesthesia. The anesthesia keeps the dog still so that the veterinarian can clean below the gum line, and it provides pain control. If you need a little more encouragement to have this done, remember that periodontal disease is painful, and chronic pain can change your dog's behavior and temperament.

Mixed-breed dogs who have dental problems should have professional cleanings done on an as-needed basis. Toy breeds in particular are prone to dental problems because their small mouths must still accommodate the same number of teeth as a German Shepherd/St. Bernard mix. Keep a strict eye on the teeth of your dog, particularly if he's tiny, no matter what mix is in his background.

Good grooming can affect your dog's mood and health. You are more likely to touch a clean dog than a dirty one, so clean dogs usually get more physical affection, too. Most of all, just sitting and brushing or combing your dog is a bonding experience you don't want to miss.

6

TRAINING and BEHAVIOR

of Your Mixed Breed

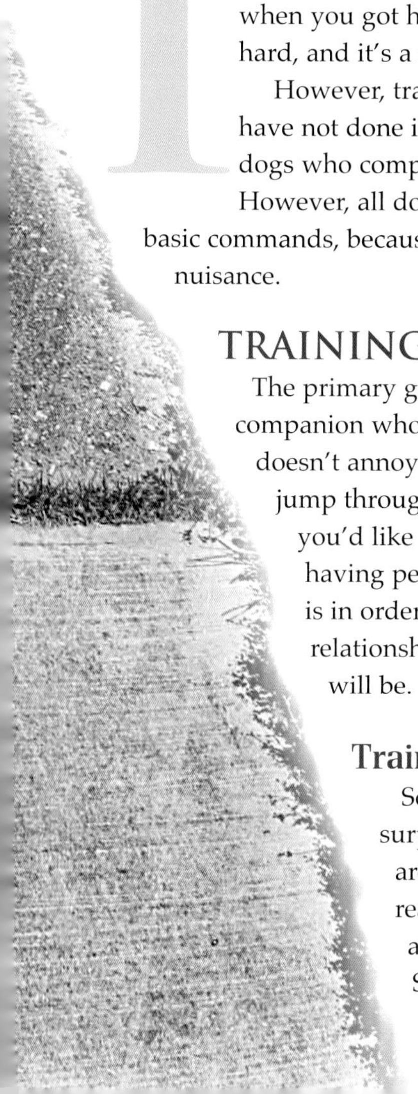

I f this is your first dog or your first puppy after inheriting your mother's ten-year-old Lab who moved at the speed of a turtle with a broken leg when you got him, you'll be thrilled to know that training a dog isn't hard, and it's a fun bonding experience shared by the two of you.

However, training can be an intimidating concept to those who have not done it before. Some people think that it's only necessary for dogs who compete in performance events like obedience or agility. However, all dogs should learn crate training, housetraining, and the basic commands, because they will make living with your pet a joy instead of a nuisance.

TRAINING BASICS

The primary goal of training is for you to end up with a canine companion whom you can live with—one who isn't out of control, doesn't annoy the neighbors, doesn't shred the house, and who doesn't jump through the screen door to teach the letter carrier a lesson. If you'd like to be able to take a walk in the neighborhood without having people joke "Who is walking whom?" then a little training is in order. The more that you train in the very beginning of your relationship with your dog, the easier the rest of your time together will be.

Trainability of Your Mixed Breed

Some dogs are easier to train than others, but the real surprise is that it's not necessarily the smarter dogs who are more trainable. Sometimes it's just the opposite—the really intelligent dogs can outsmart many people and be as hard to train as those with the really low doggy IQs. Sometimes not-so-bright dogs are easier to train. The dogs who love to please people are usually a breeze to train,

Understanding your dog makes training easier—this "play bow" means he's ready for fun!

but the independent stubborn ones can be more of a challenge. Nonetheless, any dog can be trained.

Trainability isn't based on intelligence. Rather, trainability relates to what the breed was bred to do. It's far easier to train a Border Collie/Australian Shepherd mix to keep your family together on a walk than to train a Beagle/Pug to pull sleds. Herding and retrieving breeds are bred to follow your directions; that's why Golden Retrievers are so easily trained. A Basenji/Husky mix is smart and stubborn, potentially making it a bit harder to train. What this all means to you is that you should carefully research and select the dog who is right for you. If you already have the dog and don't know his genetic background, figure out what works best for your dog through training trial and error.

Don't Forget Who You're Dealing With

Despite such pop cultural influences as Odie, Snoopy, Marmaduke, Rin Tin Tin, Benji, Scooby Doo, and those dogs in television commercials, it's easy to forget that canines are not people. They may like to hang out on the couch with you, working toward the bottom of the popcorn bowl while watching television. They may like the same things you like and enjoy the same company and walks in the woods that you do. But don't be fooled by those big eyes. Dogs are dogs, not people, and as such, you must understand how your dog thinks if you're going to successfully train him.

Doggy behavior is either instinctive and thus a reaction—not a forethought—or learned through experience. The more that you know about dog behavior, the better you will be able to train your dog to do what you want. Do your research; read some books, cruise the web, and look for pamphlets at the vet's office. And remember, dogs are not people, just as people aren't dogs. Understanding the difference between the two species and how they interact can help you be a better trainer.

Be the Leader

Dogs need a leader—they must know who to look to for direction. If you don't fulfill that role, your dog will try to do so.

You can use food rewards to train your dog.

The nature of dogs in a pack is that they all respect the chain of command and follow the top dog. It is in their nature to challenge that position once in a while and get promoted. At all times in the dog–human pack, though, *you* are the one who should be the alpha, no matter what positions your dogs have. Their positions may change, but yours can't, or they will take over and you'll all be unhappy.

As the alpha person in the household, you are the provider of resources, food, cuddling, and walks. You may bring some less-than-eagerly-anticipated events, such as going to the vet, but you also dispense treats, feed breakfast, give kisses, and lavish lots of praise. In other words, tell your by your actions that you are large and in charge. To maintain your alpha position, always ask your dog to do something, such as a simple *sit* or *stay*, before he gets anything, including meals and toys. This isn't just during puppyhood, but for life. Dogs need to acknowledge, at all stages of their lives, that you are in charge.

No Free Rides

Right off the bat, your dog needs to learn that nothing in life is free, and he has to learn that you are the leader and he is the follower. All good things come from you, including meals, toys, and petting. You are the one who provides resources, and your dog needs to understand that the provider is the one in charge. Before he gets to eat that treat, he must do what you want: sit if you say so, stop barking, stop running, or whatever it is that you ask him to do. Never give your dog the treat if he's not doing what you ask.

By being in charge, you can help pushy, barky dogs calm down and shy dogs become bolder, because dogs are more comfortable when their human is the true leader. They don't have to worry about who is making decisions, or if their leader is capable of making the right decisions.

Reward, Reward, Reward!

Positive reinforcement is about reward-driven behavior. When you reward your dog for doing what you want, he will do what you want to get the reward. Unlike some other styles of dog training, positive reinforcement does not use punishment to correct behavior—no alpha rolls, no rubbing noses in urine (as if that ever worked), or hitting with rolled-up newspapers. If you find your dog sitting, or if he sits when you ask him to, you reward that behavior. Punishment has nothing to do with it.

It's a Family Affair

If you live alone, you and only you are going to provide training. However, when your dog lives with a family, everyone needs to be involved and responsible; even small children need to learn what is acceptable and what isn't.

Trouble begins in family paradise when your dog figures out—and he will—that he can get away with something with Dad that Mom won't tolerate. As instinctive as small children, dogs will figure out who is the softie and who is the disciplinarian. While dogs love routine and discipline, it is in their nature to keep checking to see who is in charge, and if they see any viable opening in leadership, they'll make a run for it.

Furniture

Before your dog sets one paw inside your house, decide whether or not he's allowed on the furniture. Make sure that everyone in the family understands. If you decide that he should not be on the furniture, don't let him up at all, not even for a minute, because mixed signals are much harder for a dog to deal with and understand. Dogs need consistency and routine.

SOCIALIZATION

Socialization means getting a dog used to meeting a variety of new dogs and people, and going to many different types of places so that he becomes confident with new and changing situations. Socialization is the best way to provide your puppy or rehomed adult with a good start in life with you. The more variety a puppy is exposed to, the more confident that puppy will be as an adult. It's not just genetics at work here; sufficient exposure to as much of the outside world as possible goes a long way toward forming confident adults.

How much your dog likes meeting new people has a component in genetics. For example, your German Shepherd Dog mix may always be a one-person dog and never care much about meeting and greeting new people. Golden Retriever mixes, on the other hand, will generally be people oriented.

Why Is Socialization Important?

Socialization early on will shape your mixed breed's life significantly. Of course, you may find some adult dog who was neglected or abused, and who will never entirely regain trust of people or new environments, but the more that your dog

Socialization begins with a puppy's littermates.

117

is exposed to, the easier it becomes for that dog to experience anything new.

Puppies learn a lot from their mother and their littermates. Singletons or puppies removed too early from the litter may have lifelong issues interacting with other dogs because they missed a critical timeframe of interaction; littermates learn to socialize with people as a group. As adults, puppies taken from their litters too soon are either shy or aggressive. It's best for a dog to meet a variety of people, including children, at a young age.

How to Socialize

Because the point of socializing is to provide frequent exposure to many different scenarios, some people set a goal of one new experience per day for a puppy. Interactions with dogs who you already know and trust are a good choice when a puppy is quite young, particularly before he has finished the entire vaccination series. Stop and chat with neighbors while on walks, go for walks with people who are also walking their dogs, go to the park, or stop at an ice cream stand and let people fuss over your dog. Ride around in different cars. Stand outside the grocery store while waiting for someone. When your puppy is old enough, take him to puppy class and obedience school. The more good experiences that your dog has, the more confident he will be.

Socialize your mix with many different types of dogs.

When to Socialize

Socialization is most necessary from around 7 to 14 weeks of age. A puppy's fear stage usually begins around the age of 8 to 10 weeks and lasts until the puppy is about 12 weeks old. Note that these timeframes of socialization and fear overlap. After 14 weeks of age, wizened puppies become more suspicious than they were; if they've been well socialized, they'll be more confident as adults than they would be otherwise. Even outgoing puppies can become nervous and fearful during the fear stage, so during

that timeframe, make certain that you socialize your puppy to new people, dogs, places, and activities. However, control the interactions as much as you can to ensure that they are all positive. For example, take your puppy to a playdate with one vaccinated dog that you know and trust. Places like the dog park can introduce him to unsavory experiences,

If you don't provide a crate, your mix will probably look for a den-like place to hide.

and so that's not a good choice during the fear stage. It's better to introduce your puppy to one person at a time instead of several.

Puppy Class and Play Dates

Puppy class is an excellent idea, and trainers highly recommend it, although some veterinarians have concerns about exposing puppies to other dogs before becoming fully vaccinated. However, one way to approach the situation is to make frequent playdates for your puppy with dogs who you know are vaccinated and who like puppies. These dogs don't have to be puppies themselves, just dogs who like puppies.

The need for dogs to socialize doesn't end at maturity, but when your dog is an adult, you just don't need it to be as varied. Playdates don't have to be formal events, either; socialization happens when you take walks around the neighborhood and when you take him to a dog park. Even in their senior years, dogs need socialization along with those naps.

CRATE TRAINING

In the United States, crate training is seen as a beneficial tool. In fact, the crate is viewed as a major tool for housetraining, a good place to feed a dog, and a safe place for a dog to stay when his owner is not at home or when he is recuperating from illness or surgery. It's also used as a den in which dogs can have some alone time. Even if the crate isn't used for housetraining or feeding, most dogs are crated at some point for a short duration, such as at the groomer or when awaiting surgery at the vet. If you ever fly with a dog, he has to be crated, either in cargo or, for tiny dogs, under the seat in front of you. If he wanders off and is sent to the shelter, he'll be crated there while he waits for you. If you get evacuated because of a natural disaster or other such emergency, a crate is the safest place for a dog so that he won't bolt and become lost. Many people use crates in the car for safety purposes, particularly people who travel regularly to dog shows and events. Using a crate during a puppy's teething stage can protect your belongings as well as his safety—if he's in his crate, he can't swallow things while you're not home. Even if he's not teething, if he's suffering from separation anxiety, crating can protect your shoes, books, remote controls, furniture, and so on.

Introducing the Crate

Rather than just throwing your dog into a crate for the first time for nine hours while you go to work, acclimate him by having him use the crate for short sessions while you're home so that he

A crate can be an excellent housetraining tool.

Marking

Ever wonder why dogs have to pee so often during a neighborhood walk? They're not only marking their territory, they're leaving messages for other dogs. And it's not just the males—some females mark a lot. Marking involves just a tiny bit of urine; you can see how dogs save it for the length of their walk, even when you think that there cannot possibly be one more drop left.

Marking territory is accomplished by urinating on the chosen territory and is a way of establishing that the dog was there. In other words, a dog marks a spot as a sign of ownership. Of course, when all the neighborhood dogs are going for an after dinner walk, ownership of coveted real estate can change rapidly.

Because testosterone affects male behavior, neutered males are less likely to mark.

knows that it's a safe place. He needs to get used to it and see it as a comfortable place. Here's how to do it:

1. Start by situating the crate in an area that the whole household frequents, such as the family room.
2. Encourage your dog to enter by tossing some small treats near the outside of the door, then just into the crate past the door, and then throw the treats all the way to the back of the crate. Do not force your dog to go in the crate; he'll acclimate much better and faster if he thinks that it's his idea.
3. Praise him when he goes in.
4. Repeat this process a few times, and then leave him in the crate for about ten minutes.
5. Give him the command you've selected to tell him it's time to go into the crate, such as "Max, crate" or "Kennel up." Use a treat to lead him into the crate as you give the command. Close the door after he goes into it.
6. Once he lasts for 30 minutes in the crate with you in the other room and with no problems, begin crating him while you leave the house for short periods of time.

Do not get emotional during either your coming or going while your dog is crated. Displaying any emotion will only increase his anxiety or possible dislike of the crate. Staying calm and unemotional while coming and going will be easier on both of you.

How Long to Crate

A crate is a great tool that should never be used beyond its appropriate capacity. Even for dogs who don't mind crates, being crated for a work day and then allowed out at dinnertime for an hour and then crated again while you go out for the evening is unfair to the point of being inhumane, particularly if done quite regularly.

A crate is useful as long as it's not used too much, and that's where the trouble comes in. Overcrating can cause problem behaviors, and some dogs are more susceptible to those problems than others.

Dogs shouldn't be crated for more than your work day. Puppies, however, shouldn't be crated for more than three or four hours at a stretch; their little bladders just can't handle more. Dogs left crated too long for years on end have significant psychological damage, such as obsessively/compulsively twirling rather than walking because they haven't been allowed to walk enough. No movement for hours on end is bad for dogs physically and mentally.

Hopefully, when your dog reaches adulthood, gets enough daily exercise, and mellows out from his childhood mania, you can leave him uncrated in the house all day so that he can stretch out and walk around and not chew door molding or your slippers. When you think you're at that point, leave him in the house for a short period of time, such as five minutes, and run back in to see if he's being destructive. If he hasn't ruined anything, keep increasing the amount of time during which you trust him alone.

Did You Know?

Puppies usually need to eliminate right after feeding and immediately upon waking up.

HOUSETRAINING: "CLEAN UP ON AISLE 4!"

More so than any other aspect of sharing your life with a dog, housetraining is important. From our perspective, there should never be any dog urine or feces inside the house. It's disgusting, it smells bad, and it's potentially harmful in terms of health. More than that, having to clean up dog messes inside the house can ruin your relationship with your dog in a short time, and far too often, that means it's off to the shelter or shipped to another home.

Dogs, on the other hand, don't understand why housetraining is so important to humans, and they probably think that we're nuts for insisting on something so absurd. Dogs see no valid reason not to eliminate in the house except that you don't like it, even though there are several rooms and corners in which to go that are quite convenient and don't require a doorman. The good news is that at eight weeks of age, a puppy's learning capacity is in high gear, and even though he won't understand *why* you don't approve of pottying in the house, he will soon gather that you don't like it, and that will be enough for him.

Housetraining a Puppy

Before you begin housetraining, remember that puppies have tiny bladders. They need to be about 16 weeks of age before they can have reasonable control of their bodily functions. Small-breed puppies have really small bladders, and no matter what, they cannot hold it for hours upon end until they are old enough to have some control over their bladders. Even large-breed puppies are not going be housetrained right off the bat.

When housetraining your puppy, stay in the same room with him any time that he is awake. Keep an eye out for signs that he has to eliminate; most dogs will start to circle or sniff around looking for a "good" spot just before they go. Select the phrase you're going to use to tell him it's time to go, such as "Go potty." Only use that phrase when you are outside and at the spot that you want the puppy to use. Don't say it indoors or even while escorting your puppy outside. When he eliminates in the correct place, praise him up and down, kiss his head, and gleefully proclaim what a good boy he is. Give him a treat. When he goes where you want

Reward your puppy when he eliminates in the proper place.

Housetraining for Indoors

Some people like to first train their dog to use newspaper or scented piddle pads in the house and then move outside. The problem with this approach is that you have to train twice and eliminate the first training when you want your dog to eliminate outdoors only. It's easier to just start with outside training, although if you live in a high-rise apartment, getting outside quickly is a real problem, so using the paper method may work well for you.

Some people have had success using cat litter boxes with special dog litter, but this is only appropriate for toy dogs who can turn around inside a litter box. Typically, toy breeds dislike going outside in inclement weather; they are so small that they are more affected by the weather than larger dogs. Many people plan to have their tiny dogs go inside all the time using a litter box, newspaper, or piddle pads, but be aware that once you begin this method, it's nearly impossible to have the dog eliminate outdoors.

him to go, whether it's just outside anywhere or on a specific bit of ground, praise him to high heavens *as he goes*, not after.

Schedule your puppy's eating and drinking times when housetraining so that he will be prone to eliminate on a schedule. Once you've figured out his typical elimination times, housetraining will be easier. Especially that first week while he's learning, take him outside approximately once an hour and praise him if he goes. Some dogs take longer than others to learn, and smaller dogs need more time than big dogs to achieve muscular control of their elimination systems.

Housetrain a dog with positive reinforcement rather than screaming "Oh gosh, no!" at the top of your lungs as you bolt rapidly toward the dog you have just frightened into eliminating more. All dogs, even the rocket scientists, will make some mistakes.

Some toy breeds are notoriously difficult to housetrain; part of it is because they have such tiny bladders, part of it is that they are really stubborn, and part of it is that oftentimes people treat them like little princesses instead of little dogs.

Housetraining an Adult

If your new-to-you dog is an adult, you may find that he is in need of a housetraining refresher course or was never housetrained at all. Use the same approach with an adult dog that you would with a puppy. Apply positive reinforcement only; most dogs do not respond well to negative reinforcement, and the old "rub his nose in it" is not only ineffective but inhumane. The nice thing about training an adult dog is that he already has control of his muscles and can hold it, unless he suffers from a medical condition.

Accidents

When those inevitable accidents happen, do not yell at your dog. He can't help it. As tiring as it can be to clean up accident after accident, if you yell at him, he will only learn to be afraid of you. And if you yell at him minutes or hours after the incident, he will never connect the two and he will be confused, wondering what on earth you are upset about.

If your dog has an accident, clean it up quietly. Use an enzyme cleaner to eradicate the odor so that he doesn't eliminate there again.

LEASH TRAINING

Dogs must be leash trained for many reasons. Most cities have leash laws, and you can be fined for letting your dog off leash. Even if you live in a rural area, your dog will sometimes have to go where there are people and other dogs, such as the lobby of the vet clinic, where a leash is necessary. Most of all, a leashed dog is far safer than an unleashed one, because he is less likely to bolt away from you and be hit by a car. Even though dogs may be under the mistaken impression that leashes are tools of canine oppression, it is up to you to show your pet that this is not the case.

Leash training will make taking walks with your mix a pleasure.

How to Leash Train

Puppies first need to adjust to a collar. After putting one on for the first time, distract your dog with a toy or treat. Some puppies fight the collar and keep fussing with it as though it were a nylon ear infection, but if you take it off while he is still making a fuss over it, he'll think—correctly—that if he just keeps fussing, it will eventually go away. Unless there is a medical problem such as a collapsing trachea (which you will know if pulling gently on the collar causes him to cough in reaction), he'll eventually get used to it.

After your puppy is comfortable with a collar, it's time to add the leash. Feed your dog while he's wearing both the collar and leash so that he knows that good things happen when the leash is out. Let him drag the leash around for a while. After that, put the leash in your hand and let your dog know that you are now connected by gently moving it. Keep the leash as loose as possible; pulling on it creates unpleasant walks for you, and it's tough on canine throats, particularly for small dogs.

Keep your puppy's training session to five minutes at a time.

If (or more likely, when) your dog pulls the leash while walking, either stop the walk or straighten your arm and turn around. It's okay to stay in a 10-foot (3-m) circle at the end of your driveway for half an hour, no matter what your neighbors think. If you give in and walk while he is pulling the leash, you will have even more work to do to correct the behavior. Occasionally give your dog a treat when he is moving in the direction that you want to go, without pulling.

For a new-to-you adult, or for an adult in need of Remedial Leash Walking 101, use the same approach, although it may take longer. Changing directions usually works even better for adults. Get excited and happy, and ask your dog to follow you. Give lots of treats and verbal praise. Later, he will see that the leash frequently translates into a fun walk, and the benefit will be clear to him.

SIT, STAY! THE BASICS OF OBEDIENCE

The whole point of teaching basic obedience is to have a companion with whom you can easily live. No one wants to live with a dog who is out of control, barks all the time, chews shoes, and annoys the neighbors. Some people may tolerate it because training seems like too much bother, but in reality, the time that it takes to train your dog is far less than the time you would spend cleaning up after an untrained dog.

Young puppies are unable to concentrate on any one thing for very long, so keep their training sessions to five minutes at a time. Their attention spans aren't exactly in existence yet. The adult dog is able to concentrate better and can have longer training periods, but at the same time, you don't want him to become bored. It's better for any dog to have several short five-minute training sessions a day than one half-hour session.

Keep in mind that some dogs can be trained quickly, and some can't. Not every dog will learn a new command after just a few tries. It takes patience, because every dog learns at his own pace, just like human students.

Finally, training treats are a must, particularly for food-motivated dogs. Use the smallest sized treat possible so that you can use more treats without giving too many calories at once. To dogs, more treats is better than less treats. Change the types of treats to increase the excitement and reward. Some dogs like small dry treats, some prefer freeze-dried liver, some prefer certain flavors, and some like different types of meat or flavorings. What

Getting your dog to pay attention to you is one of the first steps in training.

type of treat you use doesn't matter nearly as much as whether or not your dog likes it, so use whatever you know your dog likes.

Precede Commands With Your Dog's Name

During training sessions and in general usage, commands should always be preceded with your dog's name, not the other way around. Get his attention first, and then tell him what you want. For example, say "Max, sit," rather than "Sit, Max!" It has to be clear that you are giving him a command and that he is the one to whom you are speaking.

Pay Attention

Puppies are quite easily distracted, as are some adult dogs. One of the first things you want to teach your dog, then, is to pay attention to you.

Finding a Good Dog School

Ask other dog people where they go for training classes and what they liked best and least about either their specific instructor or the school. Even though your mixed breed isn't accepted by the AKC, your local AKC dog kennel club can still provide a good recommendation for your dog, and it might accept him in a class. Your local shelter should have some ideas too.

Ask the training schools in your area if you can attend a session without your dog to see how the classes work and if you like them.

How to Teach Pay Attention

To teach this command, have treats on you, but don't let your dog see them. Start by saying your dog's name and stepping away from him. When he looks at you, praise him both with your voice and with a tasty treat. He will soon learn to pay attention to you whenever you say his name. Select places with differing distractions, such as the backyard, the dog park, or the pet supply store. By doing so, your dog will learn to focus on his alpha: you.

Sit

Sit is the easiest behavior to teach because you can use your dog's natural inclination to do it. That's part of the reason why it's usually the first behavior taught.

How to Teach Sit

Hold a treat at your dog's nose level. As his head and neck move forward to take it, pull your hand up right over his head while you say "Max, sit." The physical movement of raising his head to see the treat will make his back end drop into a sit. The absolute *moment* he sits, give him the treat while praising him enthusiastically. Repeat three times, remembering to praise him to the skies when he performs the command correctly.

Reinforce this useful command by having your dog sit for dinner, treats, while you put on his leash, and before you go out the door.

Down

Dogs like to lie down well enough to do it on their own, but being told to get into this vulnerable position is a different matter. While some of their initial reluctance has to do with physical comfort ("What do you mean, change position? I like the one I'm in!"), some of it is psychological, because the *down* is a submissive position in the dog world. You should reach the *down* after your dog has mastered the *sit*.

How to Teach Down

Tell your dog to sit and then hold your hand so that he can see the treat in it. His excitement level and interest will perk up the moment he sees the treat. Lower your hand to the floor in front of his legs, say "Max, down," and slowly pull your hand backward until he has stretched out into a *down* position.

Another method is to kneel on the ground next to your dog while he is sitting. Facing him, put your left hand over his right foreleg and your right hand over his left foreleg. Very gently pull his legs toward you while saying "Max, down."

You may find that your dog responds best to a combination of the two approaches. Whatever you do, don't force him into this position. With either approach, talk to him quietly and pet him once he is lying down to teach him that good things happen in this position. Praise and tasty treats will help to convince him that this slightly unnatural position is acceptable.

At first, only ask your dog to stay for a few minutes at a time.

Stay

Learning to stay in one place until you release a dog is important. It allows him to compose himself and remain calm even when he's excited. When company comes over, you can put him in a stay, and he won't be all over them, or he'll be calm when strangers pet him or the vet examines him. You also can keep him away from the stove while you're cooking or away from the baby while you're changing diapers, and still keep an eye on him.

How to Teach Stay

After your dog has learned the *down*, teach him how to stay. Put him in a *down* and say "Max, stay." If he starts to get up, repeat your command to stay. You may need to do this

Release Words

Whatever word you choose to use to release your dog from a command, use it consistently. Say it at the end of the exercise or when it's acceptable to you for him to get up and wander about the house. This is a case where consistency is quite important. Most people use "okay" or "all right." The problem with "okay," though, is that our daily conversations are peppered with it, and it might be confusing for the dog to know when it's a command for him and when you're not talking to him. The one word that you want to avoid as a release is "good" or whatever word it is that you use to praise him.

several times. Once he has stayed for a few seconds, praise him, give him a treat, and then let him get up. Keep repeating this as long as it takes for him to stay for five minutes. Don't let him get up until you've told him that's what you want him to do.

Next, it's time to ask him to stay when you're not right next to him. Put your dog in a *stay* and move to the other side of the room. Start with a short period of less than a minute, and then increase the duration. As you increase your distance, increase the amount of time until you're up to five minutes. Then, switch to a *sit* command and repeat the process.

Stand

The *stand* is a good behavior for a dog to know because it's very helpful on the vet's exam table; it's particularly useful for those dogs who will have to spend time on a grooming table (typically those with coats that do not shed and must be cut).

How to Teach Stand

Whatever position your dog happens to be in, hold out a treat to him, say "Max, stand," and raise it slowly to the height where your dog's face will be when he stands up. Any red-blooded dog will want that treat and stand up to get it. Give him the treat the moment he's standing.

Heel

Heeling is called *heeling* because the dog is supposed to walk next to your left heel. It doesn't really matter on what side of you your dog walks, but if you plan to go out for formal obedience training or competition, he will have to walk to your left. In agility and rally, however, being on either side of the handler is necessary, so if you wish to go out for these sports, get your dog used to walking on both sides of you. If your competition interest is strictly in obedience, though, keep your dog heeling on your left.

How to Teach Heel

Keep the leash loop in your right hand, but hold it and control it with your left hand, placing your hand about halfway down the length of the leash and leaving a bit of slack. Start by keeping a little treat in your left hand. Your dog will understand that staying close is responsible for his getting some lovely rewards, such as a treat and praise. Reward him when he walks calmly at your side, not in front of you or behind you. When you stop walking, ask him to sit.

Come (Recall)

This command is critical; in fact, no other single behavior is as important as having your dog come when he is called. It could

Teach come *in a secure, fenced area.*

Body Language

Dogs often show more than one movement to display what mood they're in. Here is a key to some of those moods:

Aggressive: A dog is feeling aggressive when his mouth and lips are open, he exposes his teeth in a grimace, his ears are nearly flattened, his body is tense and his hackles (hair along the spine) are up, he's growling, and his tail is straight out. Stay away!

Anxious: The ears on an anxious dog will be partially down but not flattened; he will whine but not growl, and his eyes will be slightly narrowed. An anxious body is tense, lowered into a somewhat submissive position, and the tail is lowered a bit.

Alert: Alertness can escalate into aggression rather rapidly, but it's still a step down from it. The ears will be up and the mouth will be slightly open. He might be standing on tiptoe, and the tail will be up and wagging slowly.

Fearful: The ears will be flat against the head, as it is with an aggressive posture, and the dog will not look directly at you. The lips are drawn back so that you can see his teeth. He'll be tensely crouched into a submissive position with his tail between his legs. This fearful posture is often accompanied by a low vocalization of some type.

Friendly: The ears will be up, with lips relaxed and eyes wide open. He'll look at you directly. His hind end may wiggle in greeting, and his tail will be up. He'll smile, and whether or not you see teeth, the jaw will be slack and relaxed.

Playful: The body will be in a similar state of relaxation as with the friendly posture, but he will be more active. The common posture is the *play bow*, in which his hind end is up in the air and his front legs are extended forward so that the shoulders are low. The tail will be wagging in excitement. He may circle around and then run forward and back as part of his invitation to play.

save his life before he runs into traffic, it could save you tears when you've just watched him run off through the woods, and it can save him from getting lost or being bitten by an injured animal. A *sit* position is nice, but it's not likely to save his life.

For this command to work, you want your dog to associate good things with coming when called. This means that when you call him, he must get a treat, not a nail trim or a pill. *Never* punish him after you've called him to you; if you do, he will never have a reliable recall.

How to Teach Come

Start by working in one room, because the small space makes it easy. Call your dog by name, and show him that you have a treat. When he walks over to you, praise him enthusiastically. (Don't reach out to him, especially if he's shy or timid. If he's shy, kneel down to be on his level.) If he is reluctant despite the odiferous treat you are proffering, put a leash on him, say "Max, come," and slowly and gently pull the leash toward you. Don't jerk the leash.

When he starts taking steps toward you, praise him to the skies, but don't offer a treat until he's actually at your feet.

When your dog comes to you reliably in a room, move outdoors to a fenced area. If you don't have a fenced yard, try to find a fenced area that you can use, such as a training area or dog park. Keep your dog on a short leash and repeat the previous steps. When his outdoor recall on a short leash is reliable, step it up a notch and use a longer leash (not a flexi), and slowly step away from him while calling him. He will soon understand that this is just an extension of what he's done before.

Practice frequently and regularly, several times a day. Then, step up the difficulty level by increasing the amount of distractions. When your dog comes to you when called, despite other dogs, kids, and somebody's roast beef sandwich and mesquite-flavored chips on the park's picnic table, you know that your dog has a reliable recall.

Leave It

A potentially life-saving command, *leave it* means that the dog is not supposed to touch, eat, or chase something that he's interested in. Given that a few ibuprofen tablets can kill a small dog, you want to be able to stop your pet from ingesting them the moment

Some problem behaviors can have medical causes—check with your vet.

you see him chewing over the open bottle.

How to Teach Leave It

Find a training object that you want him to leave alone, but don't use his toys or a treat. In fact, in the beginning, help him out by not using something he loves. And don't use food because you will want to give him very good treats when he is successful. Then, put your dog on a short leash so that you can control the situation. (Make sure that the leash is short because you want to stop him from getting to the off-limits object.)

Let's say that you're going to use an old slipper that smells like you. While your dog is on the leash, put the slipper down near you. When he starts to go toward the slipper, say "Max, leave it!" and walk away with him, using the leash. When he looks at you instead of the object, treat him and praise him. Keep repeating this process. Eventually, you'll get to the point where you don't need treats, but always remember to praise him.

If you discover that your dog has grabbed the object anyway and growls at you when you try to take it away, don't yank it out of his mouth. You could get bitten. If he shows signs of aggression

After basic training, you can move on to advanced sports like agility.

Exercise is essential for a physically and mentally happy dog.

over food or toys, consider calling a behaviorist before the issue becomes out of control.

WORKING OUT PROBLEM BEHAVIORS

Some canine behaviors, such as digging or barking, are seen by dogs as perfectly natural, while people tend to view those behaviors as a nuisance. Each time there is a problem, look at it from the dog's point of view and try to work with the behavior in canine terms. It's easier for you to understand canine behavior than it is for your dog to understand why many of his "natural" behaviors are unacceptable.

Many problem behaviors are related to lack of exercise or boredom. The more exercise and socialization your dog gets— meaning the less bored he is—the better off he'll be. A tired dog is a good dog. If you want your pet to calm down, give him a lot of daily exercise. Don't assume that playing in the backyard will take care of that need because it won't. It's just not enough. Off leash play in a fenced area, like a dog park, or long leashed walks every day will make a positive difference. Twenty minutes around the

Punishment

Just say no to punishing your dog. Punishment includes hitting your dog with your hand or an object like a newspaper, yelling, kicking, screaming, throwing things at him, rubbing his nose in urine and feces to "teach him not to do it," and so on. If you find that your dog has pooped on your new living room carpeting, yelling at him two minutes or four hours after he's done it is not going to make any sense to him. Hitting him is useless and cruel; he won't connect it with soiling the carpeting and it will just cause him to be fearful of you.

Positive reinforcement is best for training, and that involves not punishing a dog. Most dogs do not respond well at all to negative input. If your dog chews your shoes to shreds because he's nervous when you are gone, screaming at him for it when you get home will cause him to be nervous and seek more stress relief, which is likely to be more chewing. It's quite a cycle, and punishment will just perpetuate it and make things worse.

block once every other day simply is not enough to keep most adult dogs happy, and it's far too little for a puppy's physical needs.

Aggression

While there are many reasons why dogs become aggressive toward people or other dogs, it simply cannot be tolerated and must be dealt with. For one thing, it is a leading cause of euthanasia, but there is a difference between a dog who is so aggressive that euthanasia is the only choice and one who just hasn't been trained.

Liability is a frightening and significant matter, particularly in this day and age of breed-specific legislation and breed bans. Legally, your dog is your property, and you are responsible for his actions. If your pet kills another dog or mauls a child's face or even kills someone, *you* are responsible, not the dog. In view of this, aggression must be nipped in the bud and dealt with. If the unthinkable happens, your dog could be legally euthanized against your will.

Your behavior matters a great deal in your dog's level of aggression. If you are the leader, your dog will not challenge you as he would someone else. Dogs use aggressive behavior toward people to gain and maintain power, so keeping your dog in his place in the family pack can help to prevent aggression. For example, don't allow your puppy to bite or mouth you in play. If you have a dog who wants to be alpha in the household, don't let him sleep on the bed, only feed him after you've eaten, and do not play aggressive games with him, such as tug-of-war.

What to Do

If you see signs of aggression beginning in your dog, such as growling over food, growling when you take a toy away, and being highly reactive to other dogs, contact a dog trainer or canine behaviorist immediately. Some aggression issues can be dealt with effectively more easily than you might imagine, but getting help from a professional and possibly preventing it from becoming a real problem is your best bet.

Barking (Excessive)

Barking can be a significant problem with some dogs, and sadly, it is a leading reason for dogs to be given away to shelters. Barking is an instinctive behavior, although some dogs are "barkier" than others. For example, terrier mixes bark a lot, while most sighthound mixes don't bark nearly as much. But it's a rare dog who doesn't bark at all.

Unfortunately, barking is a behavior that affects your neighbors, who have every right to complain if the noise is out of control.

Excessive barking may be a sign of boredom.

Too much time alone and not enough exercise can cause problems.

You wouldn't want to try to sleep next door to a dog who barked most of the night or work from home across the street from a dog with separation anxiety who barked all day. It's not fair to your neighbors, who are acting appropriately when they call the police for excessive barking.

What to Do

When dealing with a barking issue, first try to understand why your dog is engaging in this behavior. Is he bored? Does he have separation anxiety? Is there construction going on next door with confusing noises? Also, try to separate alarm barking that has a reason from the barking that goes on because dinner isn't served yet.

There are ways to get your dog to bark less, but keep your expectation realistic—asking a terrier to stop barking entirely is an unrealistic goal. If the neighbors are calling the police, get on top of the situation immediately by contacting a behaviorist. If the problem is annoying just to you, try a different approach. When your dog barks, back away from him and then call him to you. When he comes to you and isn't barking, treat him. Soon he will realize that he's being treated for not barking. For some dogs, shaking an empty soda can with a few coins in it will work wonders to stop barking.

If you're out on a walk and your dog barks like crazy at every dog who walks by, distract him by asking him to sit, down, or stay with treats. This will stimulate his mind. Also, keep the leash loose on walks because a tight leash increases a dog's defensive response.

Chewing

Teething occurs when puppies are around four to six months of age, although some will start or stop on a different timeframe. Teething causes jaw pain, and chewing helps to relieve that pain. It's the best way that a dog has to make his jaw feel better. During this stage, people have reported awesome levels of destruction, while other puppies don't do much damage. Dogs who aren't teething can chew rather zealously to relieve stress or boredom. Smart dogs get bored easily, and they end up believing that chewing has great entertainment value.

What to Do

When dealing with puppy chewing, crating your dog when you're not home during this stage may save your shoes, couch, or marriage. Give him something to chew that's appropriate so that he won't chew on something inappropriate. Soak a washcloth in water and freeze it so that your puppy has something cold to chew on.

For only dogs who are bored, the answer may be a second dog to play with. In other cases, increasing his intellectual stimulation and exercise level can make a big difference.

Also, make sure that your dog has plenty of chew toys. When he chews something he shouldn't, trade it for one of his chew toys. If you just take the inappropriate item away, he'll want it even more than he did before, so trading is best. Let him know which things in the house are his, and try not to confuse him by giving him your old slippers, because he can't differentiate between old slippers and your favorite ones.

This is one area

Jumping up is a natural greeting for most dogs.

You're Alpha Dog

The most critical component of being alpha is to be a leader. You must be in charge, fair, and consistent in what you require. If you want your dog to dig in his own sandbox that you built for him, keep going outside with him to make sure that he isn't digging elsewhere. If you don't want him to be on the furniture, don't let him up and then change your mind after you discover that he sheds on it.

One way to maintain your alpha status is to remember that nothing is free. Everything your dog gets, such as a meal, toy, treat, or petting, should come as a result of good behavior that you've requested. (Of course, your puppy should be trained in this desired behavior first.) Ask your dog to sit before you put his food bowl down. Don't let him mouth you. And most of all, be consistent with your rules and with your training.

where your housekeeping skills affect your dog's behavior. If you would be really upset if he chewed your new red stiletto heels, do not leave those shoes anywhere he can reach them. Put them away where he cannot have access. Vigilance is key, and it's your responsibility to remove dog-attracting items out of reach. Of course, some dogs have a natural ability to get to things that you think they could never reach; this goes for tall dogs who get enough height to "counter surf" and reach that loaf of bread, or for little dogs who can jump on chairs to reach the plate of cookies on the kitchen table. Once you know that your dog can reach an item, don't leave it in that spot.

Digging

Dachshunds and terriers were bred to burrow into the ground after either rabbits or vermin, so mixes of these breeds like digging. They will always like to dig. It's a hardwired behavior, and you will not be able to entirely eliminate it. Digging does create some safety concerns; for example, a dog can dig under a fence and get out, so even if you don't care that your yard has potholes, you want to eliminate as much of that behavior as possible.

What to Do

One approach to deal with digging is to give your dog his own digging spot, or "sandbox." First, select an area in your yard where he will be allowed to dig. That's his spot, and he can dig as often and as deep as he wants. Give the area physical boundaries by fencing it with something like chicken wire or garden fencing. Cover the area with loose soil. For the next few weeks, every time your dog goes outside, go with him. Train him to dig on command in his sandbox. Let him see you plant treats or toys (or both) in the sandbox. In the beginning, don't plant them too deeply, but as you continue to train him, plant them deeper. Command him to dig for the treats by saying "Max, dig." Praise him when he uses this spot to dig. Say "No!" when he tries to dig elsewhere, walk him over to his own spot, and tell him to dig. The next step is to leave him indoors while you plant a treat and then let him find it. Remember, outdoor supervision is essential to this training.

Jumping Up

It's natural for a dog to greet people by jumping up. It's a good way to get your attention, because it brings him closer to your face (especially if he's big). Unfortunately, when you push a dog down from a jump, he views the action as a form of play, not a correction. So before he grows into an 80-pound (36-kg) jumper, train him not to do it. Even small dogs must be trained for this, or you may replace a lot of pairs of nylons and get scratched a lot.

What to Do

The trick to training your dog not to jump up is that he must have the same response from everyone he jumps on, from you to Aunt Sally to your kids and the neighbor who gives him biscuits. When he jumps, ignore him. He's looking

Sometimes dogs adopted from a shelter might develop separation anxiety.

for a response, so don't give it to him. Don't even say "Don't jump." Don't say anything, actually. Just fold your arms across your chest, turn away from him, and ignore him. This may take a long time, but eventually he will learn.

Mouthing

Puppies explore the world with their mouths. Their mouths have teeth, so they end up biting without any intention of hurting; they just do it to explore.

What to Do

When your dog puts his mouth on you, get up and walk away. If he realizes that biting is counterproductive to the attention he wants, he'll stop doing it. Don't interact with him for about a minute. Then start playing with him again as though nothing happened, but when you start playing, give him a belly rub or throw a toy for him so that he doesn't immediately return to mouthing you.

Separation Anxiety

Separation anxiety can be common in adult dogs who came from the shelter or from a rescue. As with most transplanted adults, they develop an incredibly strong bond with their people, because they know that they can be taken away from home. These dogs

Finding an Animal Behaviorist

If your veterinarian says that a given problem doesn't have a physical basis, consider using the services of a canine behaviorist. An extreme change in behavior or one that has been steadily becoming more of a problem calls for professional attention. Behaviorists have the appropriate skills to work with the psychological aspects of problem behaviors.

To find a behaviorist, contact your vet or local dog training organization. The International Association of Animal Behavior Consultants (IAABC) is a professional trade association that provides certification to animal behaviorists. IAABC's mission is to help animal owners "interrupt the cycle of inappropriate punishment, rejection, and euthanasia of animals with resolvable behavior problems." Their website has a locator service that provides a list of behaviorists by region in the United States, Canada, and Europe, although most members are American.

get stressed when left alone because they are afraid of another separation. They will follow you from room to room and want to sleep stuck on you like a barnacle because they are worried that they could lose this family, too. Sometimes dogs who have been with a family have separation anxiety for other reasons, too. Mixes of unconfident companion-breed dogs are quite prone to separation anxiety.

In a dog with separation anxiety, a distress response typically occurs about 20 to 45 minutes after being left alone. Some dogs cause damage in the house, while others cry, bark, or pace. Even though well housetrained, these dogs also can have accidents when left alone.

What to Do

If you think that your dog may be suffering from separation anxiety, do not be emotional toward him when you leave the house, because doing so will ramp up his emotional response. As you walk out the door, rather than making a fuss because you're worried about what he'll do while you're gone, just leave without talking to him. When you come back, ignore him for the first few minutes. Coming home and falling on your knees and covering him with kisses assures him that there really is a problem when you leave. No fuss, no muss: Just come and go quietly. After you've been home for five or ten minutes, then talk to him.

For short-term separation anxiety, such as when you come back from a vacation with your dog and then have to leave him to go back to work, leave clothing with your scent on it so that your dog feels comforted. Also, try keeping the television or radio on to provide white noise.

In extreme situations, people sometimes get another dog to provide company. That sometimes works and sometimes doesn't. If the anxiety is based on separation from you, rather than just being alone, adding a second dog may just make things worse, because the dog with separation anxiety may feel that he has to fight for your attention. For some dogs, however, another dog works wonders.

Don't let your puppy dig through the trash.

Doggy day care can be beneficial for dogs with separation anxiety. At these facilities, dogs get a lot of socialization and exercise, and they learn to have a good time without their people, thus reducing their emotional dependence and lessening their separation anxiety.

Call a behaviorist if your dog is so anxious that he harms himself, as by jumping through windows in your absence. She will help you find the most appropriate desensitization program for your dog. Medications are available for severe cases. However, if you can alleviate the problem with behavior modification, you can avoid possible side effects from medications, as well as the cost.

Trash Hounds

Some dogs are just born trash hounds. They love to get into the trash and eat it, strew it about, and play in it. This behavior is unpleasant to humans who have to clean up and possibly pay vet bills because of it, but for dogs, it's the equivalent of a frat party. It is a self-rewarding behavior, and once in the habit, most dogs cannot be trained not to get into the trash.

What to Do

To prevent your dog from playing in the trash, find new ways to keep it contained, such as by purchasing cans that shut and lock or by putting bricks in the bottom of a tall trash can (best for small dogs, not usually enough for large dogs), and so on. Think of it as a creative challenge. Bathroom trash should be placed out of reach, such as on the back of the toilet or on the counter.

One dangerous aspect of this behavior is that dogs will ingest anything that is appealing, and sometimes that "anything" must be removed surgically. When this occurs, playing in the trash is more than just a frustrating behavior—it's a dangerous one. This is why prevention is key.

Basic training will help your dog be a good companion. Training will also bond the two of you together and establish that you are the leader. The goal here is not to win obedience titles but to have a polite, well-behaved dog.

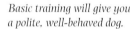

Basic training will give you a polite, well-behaved dog.

7

ADVANCED TRAINING *and* ACTIVITIES
With Your Mixed Breed

Many people devote significant leisure time to activities with their dogs, such as agility, carting, dock jumping, earthdog tests, field work, flyball, obedience, and rally, to name a few. While there are several reasons for dogs and their people to participate in any of these activities, the main reason is that it's fun. You and your dog get to spend quality time training for and participating in an activity. The other significant reason is that doing any structured activity with your dog adds to the joy of the human–animal bond. You and your dog will become closer, even though you don't feel that's possible because you're already breathing as one.

One caveat to participating in organized sports is that the governing organizations of some sports do not allow mixed breeds to participate in sanctioned competition. If you truly desire to compete in carting or lure coursing, for example, get an appropriate purebred for that sport. However, if you just want to have fun and don't care if you compete or not, or even if the activity you're considering isn't competitive, there's something out there for you and your mixed breed.

THE CANINE GOOD CITIZEN PROGRAM

While you may be surprised to see mention of the American Kennel Club (AKC) here in the context of mixed breeds, your mixed breed can (and should) participate in the AKC's Canine Good Citizen Program alongside the purebreds. This program is designed to teach owners to train their dogs to be good, livable companions with basic manners. The program emphasizes responsible dog ownership and basic obedience. It's a great way to start out training your dog to see where your interests lie and in what areas your dog is most skilled.

The program emphasizes walking under control, coming when called, staying in place, lying down, and sitting, all on command. These are basic skills that your dog will need if you are to participate in any performance event.

Correction collars such as pinch, prong, or electronic cannot be used during the test. Also, your dog should have a bath prior to the test.

The Stations

The examination includes ten separate stations.

1. **Accepting a Friendly Stranger.** The examiner will shake your hand and get close to you while your dog is next to you. The examiner will ignore the dog, who should not show any shyness or resentment toward this interaction.

2. **Sitting Politely for Petting.** Your dog should allow friendly strangers to pet him. To this end, the examiner will approach and pet him on the head and body; the dog should not show any shyness or resentment.

3. **Acceptance of Grooming.** This exercise is why you need to bathe your dog. Bring the brush you normally use, and give it to the examiner to use on your dog. (This exercise shows that your dog is able to accept veterinarians and groomers and behave appropriately.) The examiner will pick up one of the dog's feet to see if he will allow his feet to be handled.

4. **Walking on a Loose Lead.** Who is in control: you or your dog? Your dog must walk nicely on lead without pulling you all over the place. You walk around under the examiner's directions. The point is to see if your dog is attentive to you.

Passing the Canine Good Citizen test is the mark of a well-behaved family pet.

Agility is a fun sport consisting of obstacles like jumps and weave poles.

5. **Walking Through a Crowd.** Is your dog capable of walking normally through pedestrian traffic? He will walk through a group of people so that the examiner can determine whether he's paying more attention to you than them, even if they're calling him. This examination requires that your dog's focus is on you. He should not be fearful of or aggressive toward any individual.

6. *Sit* **and** *Down* **on Command and** *Stay in Place.* Does your dog respond to your commands to sit and down? During this test, you can repeat commands. (You cannot do that during formal obedience competition.) The dog has to do both a *sit* and *down*. However, while you can repeat commands, you can't touch him in any way to get him into a position. You can only talk to him.

7. **Coming When Called.** The goal is to see if your dog comes when you call him. This seems basic, but it can be a lifesaver. The dog is put on a long loose line, and you must walk 10 feet (3 m) away before calling him to you. If necessary, you can use body language and verbal encouragement. You just can't grab him by the neck and drag him as though you were a Neanderthal on a date.

8. **Reacting to Another Dog.** Two people who each have a dog approach each other, stop, shake hands, and walk away. Both dogs should stay with their person and not go to the other dog or person. The examiner wants to see if your dog reacts to the other dog or if he's polite around dogs.

9. **Reaction to Distraction.** Is your dog confident around common distracting situations? The evaluator will provide

two distractions, such as dropping a chair or having a jogger run in front of the dog. The dog can notice what's going on, but he shouldn't bark, run away, or react aggressively.

10. **Supervised Separation.** Will your dog tolerate your absence for three minutes while an examiner holds the leash? He shouldn't whine, bark, pace, or show a reaction stronger than mild agitation.

AGILITY

Agility, which debuted at the Crufts dog show in 1978, is a competitive sport that tests your training and handling skills over

a timed obstacle course. Dogs jump hurdles, run up and down ramps, whip through open and closed tunnels, walk over a seesaw, and glide through weave poles. This sport requires significant training and practice.

In recent years, agility has become hugely popular, attracting all kinds of breeds and people. Athletic dogs enjoy it, and dogs of all sizes and breeds—including mixed—can participate. You'll see a lot of Border Collies in particular, but any breed or mix can do it if they are athletic enough. It's great exercise for both you and your pet, and training to compete creates a bond because you work so closely together.

This shelter mix loves Disc Dog competitions—she never lets her "tri-paw" status hold her back!

Different organizations offer agility competitions in which mixed-breed dogs can participate, such as the North American Dog Agility Council (NADAC) and the United States Dog Agility Association (USDAA).

CAMP

For sheer fun and to dip your paws into new activities, try going to summer dog camp. Many dog camps are open in the United States. Some cater to giving you and your dog a fun vacation, while others aim to improve specific skills, such as agility camp. At some camps, you can try out several activities, such as hiking, agility, rally, tracking, tricks, and so on. Search the Internet or look at ads in the back of dog magazines.

CANINE DISC (DISC DOG)

Whether canine disc involves organized competition, hanging out with friends, or just you and your dog goofing off together at the park, throwing a disc into the air for your dog to catch is a ton of fun. The really wonderful aspect of playing canine disc is that a dog can burn off a lot of energy, and the handler only has to exert minimal physical effort to still remain in play. Australian Shepherds and Border Collies tend to be the breeds that win in this sport, but any dog who likes to catch discs in the air is welcome.

If your mix loves the water, why not try some kayaking?

One helpful tip is to have someone knowledgeable show you how to throw the disc properly. It sounds simple—kids do it all the time—but if you teach yourself some bad habits, you won't enjoy yourself as much in competition.

No one overwhelming organization exists, but fanciers participate via local clubs. The UFO World Cup Series of Frisbee is one organization that runs competitor-friendly contests. The UFO aims to organize a series of competitions that make up a World Cup Series of Frisbee dog events. The UFO works directly with Frisbee dog clubs to run the events, and individuals join clubs, not the UFO itself. Events are open to everyone. Competition includes events for freestyle routines and long-distance throws. The International Disc Dog Handlers' Association (IDDHA), a relatively new nonprofit group of members, unites individual handlers, local and regional clubs, and the dogs themselves. IDDHA recognizes levels of achievement through testing, titling, ranking, and records, and follows its own regulations. Handlers can use any disc they prefer. Their tag line is "Turning prey into play with IDDHA."

CARTING

Carting, sometimes known as drafting, dates back to the Middle Ages. Once a utilitarian activity, it's now a fun sport involving a dog pulling either an empty cart or a cart with a person. Often, a dog will pull a decorated cart in a parade or a dog jog. One dog or a *brace* (the term for two dogs) can pull the cart.

Some carting clubs are not breed specific and allow any dog, including mixed breeds, to participate. One such club is the New England Drafting & Driving Club, Inc. (NEDDC), founded in 2003. They offer training, classes, and titles. NEDDC's regulations are based on the drafting principles of the Greater Swiss Mountain Dog Club of America, Inc. (GSMDCA) and the Bernese Mountain Dog Club of America, Inc. (BMDCA). Look around for similar venues if you wish to compete, and be sure to review current rules and regulations before you start training if you wish to go for a title.

Of course, there's no reason why you can't just cart around for fun. Carting attracts a lot of attention, and the dogs feel proud and happy to be noticed, as long as they've been appropriately trained and have the right equipment.

Mixes who are part Bernese Mountain Dog, Greater Swiss Mountain Dog, Newfoundland, Saint Bernard, Bouvier, Giant Schnauzer, and Rottweiler may excel at carting.

DOCK JUMPING

Not surprisingly, dock jumping is exactly what you think it is: dogs jumping off the end of a dock into water while chasing a toy. The canine water version of the long jump, the distance that the dogs jump off the dock is measured from the point where they leap off to the point where they land in water. Needless to say, this is not a winter sport.

A team consists of one person and one dog. To participate in competition events, the dog must be at least six months old,

Understanding the Rules

Neither the AKC nor UKC is a static organization. If they were, breed clubs wouldn't be able to join, and yet new breed clubs are brought into the kennel clubs every year. Rules change from time to time, just as they do in other organizations, like professional baseball. Before you go out for your chosen sport, then, review the rules of the sponsoring organization to make sure that you remember them correctly and to see if any changes were made. The day of an event is not the time to discover that you've been training for an outdated sequence. Stay on top of your sport by reading the rules and asking questions if you don't understand them.

Good Sportsmanship Means No Whining

Sportsmanship is as important in dog sports as it is in any human sport. For dog fanciers, competitions are a way to enjoy life, not to sprawl out and whine. Spot will not understand why you are upset when you've just had a ton of fun, even if he just jumped out of the obedience ring to beg some popcorn from that nice lady sitting ringside. When you participate in dog activities, you must have a sense of humor, or you're going to drive yourself crazy, not to mention the people around you. No one likes a poor loser, and—believe this to your core—people really don't want to hear you complain endlessly.

Granted, you have to have some competitive drive or competitive events aren't going to be fun for you. But winning is not the only goal; bonding with your dog, getting out and socializing with like-minded people and dogs, having fun, and getting exercise are significant, useful goals. Only one runner can win a race, but that doesn't mean that the others can't have a good time. If you don't win this time, invest more time in preparation for the next event.

and the human must be at least seven years old. The team has 90 seconds for the dog to complete the jump from the time the cue to go is given. Jumps can reach more than 20 feet (6 m); and the distance is measured digitally.

DockDogs is the independent governing and sanctioning body for regional, national, and international dock jumping performance sports. It stipulates that a dock is supposed to be 40 feet (12 m) long, 8 feet (2 m) wide, and 2 feet (0.6 m) over the water's surface. The sport has been televised and is rapidly increasing in popularity. Mostly, people have their dogs participate in it because the dogs just love it.

Retrieving and sporting mixes will most likely have the best advantage in dock jumping.

DOG JOGS

Typically, dog jogs are fund-raisers for animal-related nonprofit groups, although some of them are meant simply to be social. A large group of people and dogs get together in the morning and walk or run for a predetermined length. Sometimes people pay a fee to participate; other times, people are asked to gather sponsors for their efforts. Even if sponsorship is not involved, participants have a fun time walking or running in a canine-oriented crowd of adults and children. Sometimes the dogs and people even wear costumes!

Dog jogs provide great incentive to walk your dog and get plenty of exercise.

DOG PARKS

Used appropriately, dog parks are some of the finest places around. Most dog parks are designed to be off leash so that your dog can run free to play and socialize. There are many kinds of dog parks, and the best ones are fenced so that dogs can't run out when you don't want them to. Many municipalities offer pick-up bags so that you don't have to drive home with a bag of poop (a particular joy on a hot summer day).

Your dog must have the right temperament to go to a dog park. This means that he should enjoy meeting other people and dogs. If your pet enjoys chomping on the hind end of other dogs, a dog park is not suitable for him. If your dog hates strangers who come up and try to pet him, a dog park will upset him, possibly enough to lead to a bite case. If you have a dog-reactive dog or an aggressive one, *do not* bring him to a dog park. However, if your dog has the right temperament, there's nothing else like it in the world. A group of dogs who didn't know each other five minutes earlier can turn into a playing pack, running around and having a good time. You and your dog will get exercise and socialization.

EARTHDOG TESTS

In an earthdog test, a dog demonstrates that he can follow game to ground and work his quarry. The dog is to follow prey into its den. Usually, the live quarry consists of two rats in a cage; the rats have food and water and are not hurt. Terriers and terrier mixes have an innate aptitude for this sport.

Dog parks can be a great place for dogs (and their owners) to socialize.

What does a dog do in an earthwork trial? He follows prey such as a rat down a tunnel and "works" it. He follows the scent of the rat into a 9 inch by 9 inch (23 cm by 23 cm) tunnel. The rat's scent is already laid out. At the end of the tunnel is the den, where the caged rats are found. The dog "works the quarry" by barking and digging; he also may growl, lunge, and bite at the cage to work the quarry.

The first competitive trial is Junior Earthdog (JE), for which the tunnel is 30 feet (9 m) long and has three 90-degree turns. The Senior Earthdog (SE) also has a 30-foot (9-m) tunnel with three 90-degree turns but adds in a false den and exit, and the owner has to call the dog out of the tunnel. The caged rats are taken out of the tunnel before the owner calls the dog. The Master Earthdog (ME) title is given for work in a 30-foot (9-m) tunnel with three 90-degree turns, one false entrance, a false den, and an exit. The dog has to go to the correct entrance and has to let another dog work simultaneously. Letting another dog work while your dog waits quietly is called *honoring* another dog; needless to say, honoring is only found at the highest level of competition.

The goal of the American Working Terrier Association (AWTA) is to encourage owners of terriers and terrier mixes to hunt in the field to maintain their working abilities. The AWTA grants certificates. A Certificate of Gameness (CG) is given to qualifying dogs in the Open Division, and Hunting Certificates (HC) are granted to dogs who participate in hunting regularly for more than a year. Working Certificates (WC) are for dogs who qualify with work in a natural den.

FIELD WORK

Sadly, the field tests and hunt trials in America only allow purebreds to compete. But that doesn't mean that you can't have fun doing the work with your sporting mix.

Pointer or setter mixes who notice a bird and literally point it out to you can learn to flush out the birds. The alleged goal of the flush is to allow the hunter to shoot the bird so that the dog can retrieve it, but if your dog just has a great time flushing and getting the birds all worked up, that's fine. Spaniel-type breeds flush in a similar fashion except they typically work closer to the hunter than do the pointers and setters. Retriever mixes are supposed to retrieve. In the field, they must figure out where the bird has

Begin With the Basics

Every competitive sport or activity requires a sound background in basic obedience, so making sure that your dog is well trained in the basics lays a solid foundation for other sports. Even if you don't wish to compete in competitive obedience, helping your dog to become proficient at following basic obedience commands is the best way to start.

landed, get it, and then bring it to you. Whistles and arm signals are used for some of this work.

FREESTYLE

Music may soothe the savage breast, but it also provides a wonderful background for a dog and person to dance to it with choreographed moves. You choose the music and design the dance steps with your dog's physical size and abilities in mind. It is both sport and entertainment, and training is good exercise for both team members. You don't need to be Fred Astaire or Ginger Rogers to participate. Competitive routines are breathtaking to watch—real crowd pleasers. It's about artistry and grace, style and image. Contact your local dog club to see who in town offers freestyle training, and start thinking about music you like.

Dogs who are active and have good basic obedience skills enjoy freestyle. Active mixed breeds, such as herding and retrieving breeds, are common participants, although any dog can take part.

FLYBALL

A sport out of California, flyball came on the scene during the late 1970s. It's a fast relay race with hurdles that is particularly well suited to dogs who love to chase balls.

A team has four dogs. One at a time, each of the four dogs leave the starting line and jump over four hurdles to reach a box at the end of the stretch. The spring-loaded box is 51 feet (16 m) away. A dog steps on the box and makes a tennis ball shoot out. He then grabs the ball, pivots around, and races back over the hurdles. After he returns to the starting line, the next dog takes off. The first team with no errors wins the heat. (The height of the hurdles is adjusted for the size of the dogs in the team so that terrier mixes don't compete with Lab mixes.)

A Pointer mix still can have fun pointing and flushing, even if he's not in competition.

Common Courtesy Isn't Common Enough

Be a considerate dog person. *Always* clean up after your dog, stand in line and wait your turn, don't scream at other participants or judges, and be ready for your event. Don't be rude about other people's dogs. Don't blame other people for your mistakes or failures. There are some folks in this world—yes, even in the dog world—who think that the rules do not apply to them because they are *special*. They have driven farther, they have trained more, and they just plain want to win more than you do, and that's what makes them special. Would you want to spend time with someone like that? Of course not. You wouldn't even let your dog spend time with them. So, however you react in the privacy of your home to the competition aftermath, be gracious at all times in public.

Always carry poop bags, use them, and dispose of them in proper receptacles. It seems like such an obvious thing, but apparently it's not. Some people think that it doesn't matter if they don't pick up that last piece of poop, but they are wrong—it does matter. Venues filled with inconsiderate dog owners eventually decide against having dog activities, so the number of venues that accept dog events decreases regularly. If you hope that your group will be welcomed back to that venue, the best approach is to pick up after your dog, and not let him bark or disturb the other patrons who have nothing to do with the dog activities.

The North American Flyball Association (NAFA) offers the following titles:

- FD, Flyball Dog
- FDX, Flyball Dog Excellent
- FDCh, Flyball Dog Champion
- FM, Flyball Master
- FMX, Flyball Master Excellent
- FMCh, Flyball Master Champion
- ONYX, ONYX Award 20000 Plaque
- FGDCh, Flyball Grand Champion
- HOBBES, HOBBES Awards

Contact NAFA to learn where and when classes are held in your area. You'll have a happy, tired dog, and as we all know, a tired dog is a good dog.

HERDING

Mixed breeds of a herding heritage—those responsibility-driven guys who nip at your heels to keep the family together on a walk—may enjoy herding competitions. Herding work means that your dog learns how to move livestock along. Typically, the livestock involved includes sheep, ducks, or cattle.

The focus of the American Herding Breed Association (AHBA) is on practical herding work, even if you don't live on a farm or have daily access to livestock. This group takes herding seriously and doesn't feel that it should be a casual hobby. The AHBA doesn't care if your dog is purebred; it just asks that he have herding instincts that you are willing to work. Their Herding Trial Program allows dogs to demonstrate herding ability in herding trials at starting, intermediate, and advanced levels on a standard course and on farm/ranch courses, which vary in detail but include specified requirements.

The AKC has a herding trial program, but it is only for purebreds.

HIKING

Sadly, American national parks do not allow dogs outside of cars, so the hiking dog fancier with an active, fit dog must find other places in which to hike together. Do some research, and find the parks and beaches that allow dogs, either on leash or off, and go for it. National forests typically have the best hiking opportunities for dogs and their people, because dogs are allowed on most national forest trails. Most national historic parks allow dogs too. Do your homework before you get in the car, though. Consult a source, such as the book *The Canine Hikers Bible*, to check out where you can take your dog hiking.

Most dogs can carry up to a quarter of their own body weight in a properly fitting dog pack. That way, they can hike while carrying their own water, food, and pick-up bags.

If you and your mix are both active, you can find a park that allows dogs and do some hiking.

LURE COURSING

Lure coursing is running races, like the track portion of track and field. Dogs chase plastic bags, not live prey, on a course designed to simulate escaping game. Mixed breeds are not eligible to compete in lure coursing events from either of the two official lure course sanctioning organizations in the United States, the American Sighthound Field Association (ASFA) and the AKC. However, if having fun is more important to you than competing, many lure coursing clubs allow mixed breeds and dogs who are

not sighthounds to participate in practice runs and fun runs. They provide these events for training and conditioning, so they do not award titles. If you wish to try this fast-paced, heart-pounding sport in which your dog burns off a ton of energy and you don't have to run, contact your local lure coursing club and ask about opportunities for mixed breeds to practice.

OBEDIENCE

Some AKC obedience events are open to mixed-breed dogs, and obedience is appropriate for dogs of all types. This is a competitive sport in which people train their dogs to perform specific behaviors.

The biggest benefit of competing in obedience is the bonding that occurs between you and your dog during training. You work-one-on one together, and your dog knows that this is his special time with you. The necessary amount of training time brings you and your dog closer than ever.

In the AKC, three levels of obedience competition are offered: novice, open, and utility. In each competition, your dog needs to score more than half of the available points (the amount differs per event but ranges from 20 to 40) and get a minimum score of 170 out of 200 possible points to pass. If your dog gets 170 or higher, he has a leg toward a title. It takes three legs for your dog to win an obedience title. The scoring system may appear confusing, but even intimidated beginners eventually figure it all out.

The Novice level earns a Companion Dog (CD) title. Skills tested include heeling both off and on leash at different speeds, coming when called, staying quietly with a group of dogs, and standing up for a physical exam. The second level is called Open, where dogs earn a Companion Dog Excellent (CDX) title. The exercises are similar to those in Novice, with jumping and retrieving thrown in for fun, but they are done off leash and for longer periods. Competitions at the Utility (UD) level perform more difficult exercises and include scent discrimination. UD dogs can work toward an Obedience Trial Champion (OTCH) and Utility Dog Excellent (UDX).

RALLY

A combination of agility and obedience, rally is the newest competitive dog sport. In it, dog and handler work a course of action selected by the rally judge, so every event is different

Conformation (Showing)

Conformation is for purebred dogs. Because the point is to see if a dog conforms well to a predefined breed standard, mixed breeds cannot participate in conformation events. Conformation is the only event in which mixed breeds aren't allowed to compete.

for your dog. The course has 10 to 20 stations, so your level of experience is taken into consideration.

Rally is more informal than obedience. Some of the steps, such as weaving or halt/sit/down, are learned in agility and obedience. Not only can you use food rewards in the ring, but you can talk to and encourage your dog. More and more people are learning to enjoy it because it has an atmosphere different from that of formal obedience.

The Association of Pet Dog Trainers (APDT) holds rally trials for mixed breeds. The team (handler and dog) runs a course of stations, as in agility, but the moves are usually combination steps from the obedience ring, such as:

- HALT–Sit –Down–Walk Around
- Left Turn
- About Turn–Right
- About "U" Turn
- 270-Degree Right (Turn)
- 360-Degree Right (Turn)

TRACKING

A dog's ability to smell is 10,000 times stronger than a human's, so any breed can learn to track a scent. Canine tracking, as a sport, consists of a dog following a person's scent trail and hopefully finding the person. More than just a sport, though, tracking is not only a way of life for many dogs, but also one that has several applications that benefit people. Tracking dogs work with police to find lost people, criminals, and drugs. Dogs also find lost pets and misplaced items.

A variety of organizations offer titles for tracking or just lessons for fun. As a sport, the events are noncompetitive in that your dog doesn't go up against other dogs—he just proves that he can or cannot do what's asked.

While scenthounds and mixes thereof excel at tracking, other dogs can have a great time tracking too. Just because they won't be hired as a professional doesn't mean that they can't enjoy it!

This Golden/Lab mix is a seeing-eye guide for the blind.

SCHUTZHUND

Tracking, obedience, and protection are the components of Schutzhund, which is a versatility test for working dogs. Mixed breeds are welcome to compete. In tracking, a dog tracks footsteps over mixed terrain and despite changes in direction. He also has to find dropped articles and indicate their locations. The obedience portion is similar to that of obedience competitions. In the protection phase, the dog must not bite the trial helper unless either the dog or the handler is "attacked" by another trial helper, in which case the dog must attack fully. Dogs compete in all three of these activities on the same day.

The United Schutzhund Clubs of America is the foremost organization. Eight titles are available.

Suitable for working breeds, German Shepherds, Belgian Malinois, Dobermans, Rottweilers, Giant Schnauzers, and Bouviers are the breeds typically associated with the sport. Other breeds or breed mixes becoming more noticeable in the sport are Belgian Sheep Dogs, Belgian Tervurens, Boxers, American Pit Bull Terriers, American Staffordshire Terriers, Airedale Terriers, Beaucerons, Dutch Shepherds, Australian Shepherds, and sometimes even Great Danes and Mastiffs. But as the sport authorities say, any breed of

Most sledding dogs prefer pulling the sled, not riding it!

dog that can do the work is welcome, although it's doubtful that you'd see any Pugs out there.

SEARCH AND RESCUE

Search-and-rescue dogs are some of the most highly skilled dogs around. They work to find people who might be buried alive in the rubble of a natural disaster or terrorist attack. They are critically important in the aftermath of earthquakes, avalanches, hurricanes, and explosions. They look for missing children, hunters, drowning victims, hikers caught in bad weather, and so on. Because these dogs walk into places that are falling apart, a bit like firefighters, it takes a truly special handler to accompany search- and-rescue dogs. Handlers are usually police officers, firefighters, or other types of first responder. These teams are real heroes.

The Search Dog Foundation (SDF) recruits dogs, including mixed breeds, from shelters and breed rescue groups, trains them, and then partners these dogs with firefighters and other first responders. All these rescue dogs are screened against the SDF's criteria and then trained. The dogs who are typically selected have the temperament that suits them to this work but that does not often suit them to being a family pet. These dogs are high energy, highly driven, tenacious, and bold, characteristics that make them a bit hard to live with as family pets.

SCOOTERING

Do you have a dog who is so hyper that he needs a ton of exercise? The idea here is to put a sled dog harness on your high-energy canine and rope the dog to a scooter. Then, you get on the scooter and ride while the dog pulls and runs until he's worn out (or until you get bored, whichever comes first). Typically, scooter dogs can run for up to 20 miles (32 km) on backcountry trails.

This activity is also a good nice-weather training exercise for sled dogs, many of whom are mixed breeds. You work together as a team, much like a musher and sled dog. The dog gets to exercise to his heart's content, and you get to bond with your dog in the beautiful outdoors.

SLEDDING

Mush! If you like winter sports, you're sure to love riding behind a sled pulled by dogs. While some people think that sled

Sports and Safety

One downside to highly active competitive events is that dogs can become injured. Safety is paramount to any competition, no matter how long you have trained or how far you have come. If your dog has sustained an injury before you leave for an event, don't go, because the injury will most likely become worse. Your dog's health is more important than any single competition. If your dog appears to limp or feel ill when you've arrived for the competition but haven't begun, the best plan is to avoid further injury and not participate. Some of these events have a veterinarian on the premises who can look over your dog, but more than anything, let common sense prevail when it comes to the safety and health of your dog.

dogs only participate in known races like the Iditarod or Yukon Quest, many people just get out behind a team and have a great time goofing around. The driver and dogs in the team bond in an amazing way.

ISDRA Sled Dog Racing, an organization devoted to sled dogs, believes that they run because they love it, but how well those dogs run depends on training, and lots of it. ISDRA indicates that any dog of medium or larger size, at least 35 pounds (16 kg) or more, can be considered a potential sled dog if he has a desire to pull and please. (Note that this requires more than just the wish to pull.) Different breeds and mixed-breed dogs run as sled dogs in addition to the common Siberian Husky, Samoyed, and Alaskan Malamute. While people generally think of northern dogs as the sled racers, German Shorthair and English Pointers crossed with Alaskan Huskies are making great inroads into the sport and setting some speed records.

At least two dogs are needed to pull a sled, and that's for people who don't weigh more than 100 pounds (45 kg). If you want to get into competition, hook up with an experienced musher to learn the ropes.

SKIJORING

In skijoring, a cross-country skier and dog or dogs are connected by a harness, belt, and tugline. Almost any skis work well except for those with metal edges that can accidentally harm the dog.

Skijoring used to be wildly popular only in far-away frozen places like Scandinavia and Alaska, but the sport's popularity is growing by leaps and bounds. Unlike sled dog racing, skijoring only needs a little bit of specialized equipment and one or two dogs rather than a whole team.

Competitions typically involve sprint races anywhere from 3 to 10 miles (5 to 16 km), but there are a few endurance races of 20 and 50 miles (32 and 80 km). If you're not into competition and just like the idea of being out in the snow and woods powered by your dog, make sure that dogs are welcome on the trails you want to use.

Check with your local skijoring club for training information and event details.

Bikejoring

A subset of skijoring, bikejoring allows you to take your energetic dog biking with you. The difference between bikejoring and going for a bike ride with your dog at your side is that in bikejoring, the dog is under your control, and you work as a team. You'll need a harness for your dog(s), a bungee line, and some type of connection to the front part of the frame of your bike. The trick here is to keep the line between you and the dog from getting slack, because when it gets slack, it can get caught in the front wheel. To avoid a slack line, it takes focus and a quick reaction with the brakes to slow down when the dogs slow down.

Because it is a relatively new sport, there isn't much yet in the way of formal equipment, but that will probably change soon.

THERAPY

The best volunteer work in the world is working with your therapy dog. You and your dog get to go in to a hospital, rest home, or rehabilitation center and provide cheer and comfort to people who are not having an easy time. Together, you offer comfort, calm, and a certain level of healing that comes from the mind and spirit. Studies show that petting an animal lowers a human's blood pressure, whereas stress can interfere with healing. Petting a dog and talking to him allows people to think about something good instead of worrying about their health, even if just for a few minutes.

Just as not every dog is suited for the obedience ring, not every dog will be a good therapy dog. Most facilities prefer to recruit therapy dogs through the two nationally known dog therapy organizations, Therapy Dogs International (TDI) and the Delta Society. These groups certify dogs and then connect teams with facilities.

Not all programs or facilities require

Well-trained and socialized mixes can make excellent therapy dogs.

Competitive events aren't for everyone—spending time walking with your mix can be just as rewarding.

certification. Some programs have their own criteria and don't care if you're affiliated with one of the national groups. Some of these programs are created for specific environments, such as acute care children's hospitals.

What most programs want is an adult dog who has been screened for health, who likes people and other dogs, and who likes to be touched and petted. Dogs should be bathed before a therapy visit, and they shouldn't be hungry.

Reading Dogs

Children who have a bit of difficulty learning to read enjoy reading to therapy dogs; the dogs don't correct them, make fun of them, or get frustrated or antsy. This activity is meaningful volunteer work for both the handler and the dog. Children sit on the floor with the dogs and practice reading aloud to them. The handler can help when the child gets stuck and provide encouragement, but the point is for the child to read to the dog. The dog loves the attention, the child loves the dog, and the child gets more practice reading. This is an excellent activity for a calm older dog, and the quality of hips or health doesn't matter as much as the dog's ability to connect with a child. Breed doesn't matter at all.

To participate, find a local group that practices this work. Start by calling dog clubs, schools, and libraries, and someone should be able to point you in the right direction.

WEIGHT PULLS

Weight pulls are exactly what they sound like: a contest to see which dog can pull the most weight. It's sort of like a canine version of a tractor pull. The goal is to see which dog can pull the most heavily weighted sled for 16 feet (5 m). The handler is not allowed to have any contact with the dog during the pull, so it's truly all up to the dog.

Dogs compete only in their own weight class.

Points are earned based on a dog's completion position and the number of dogs he beats. The five best pulls are used toward the total amount of points for the season.

The type of sled used depends on the environment. On the ground, a wheeled cart is used, while on snow, the dogs pull a sled. The International Weight Pull Association (IWPA) offers sanctioned events to any healthy dog, typically during the cooler months. Sometimes these events are held in conjunction with sled races. Safety is one of the association's main concerns.

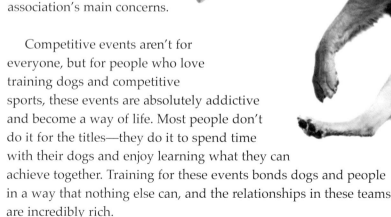

Competitive events aren't for everyone, but for people who love training dogs and competitive sports, these events are absolutely addictive and become a way of life. Most people don't do it for the titles—they do it to spend time with their dogs and enjoy learning what they can achieve together. Training for these events bonds dogs and people in a way that nothing else can, and the relationships in these teams are incredibly rich.

HEALTH
of Your Mixed Breed

Good health makes for a good quality of life in dogs as much as it does in people. Good health, however, doesn't just happen; it requires good nutrition, good veterinary care, and a measure of good luck.

ARE MIXED BREEDS HEALTHIER THAN PUREBREDS?

Does hybrid vigor, the notion that dogs who are less related have, in general, increased fertility and health, really exist? Sure. It just doesn't occur quite as often as people think because it is more than a matter of not mating the same breed. People assume that as long as the bitch and stud are different breeds, the offspring will be healthy, but that's not necessarily true—or false. As Forrest Gump would say about a box of chocolates, "You never know what you're gonna get."

Despite popular claims of hybrid vigor in all mixed breeds (see Dr. Joni Freshman's thoughts in Chapter 2), it does not occur in all dogs of this type just because they are mixed breeds. According to Dr. Freshman, hybrid vigor occurs among dogs who have the least amount of genetic background in common; they generally have increased fertility and better health than those with a common heritage. However, because you don't know the background of the mixed breed, you cannot know for sure what genetic background the dog may share. And if each of two mixed-breed parents are predisposed to the same health problems, a mixed-breed dog can have those problems, too.

In short, don't assume that because your dog is not purebred that he is going to be wonderfully healthy and never need to see the vet except for annual exams. Additionally, if you found an unidentifiable stray on the side of the road, he could have good genetics that were overridden by early malnutrition and neglect. Keep an eye out for health issues just as you would with any dog, and see your veterinarian regularly.

THE VETERINARIAN

Having a working relationship with a good veterinarian whom you trust is critical. Mixed breeds can be wonderfully healthy their entire lives, or they might need to see the vet every few months from puppyhood on.

A Good Veterinarian Isn't Hard to Find

If this is your first pet and you don't yet have a vet, or you've moved to a new area, do some research before you get your dog.

Ask Other People for Recommendations

The best way to find a good vet is to ask other people what clinic they go to and why. What do they like about that clinic or that veterinarian? Do they only like one vet, or do they recommend several? If you don't know your neighbors yet, call a local dog club or training school and ask for a recommendation.

Don't Choose Based on Price

Basing your choice of vet on price alone can be a big mistake. Let's say you call three clinics and ask what they charge to spay a five-month-old puppy. You will get a range of three prices. Before you gravitate to the low cost, though, make sure to ask what is included with the spay. Will your dog get a full physical examination prior to her surgery? What safety precautions does the clinic take? Does it use breathing tubes on all anesthetized patients? Does it have a heart and oxygen monitor or a crash box? That equipment costs money and increases the price of surgery, but it could easily save your dog's life.

Ask How the Clinic Manages Pain

One of the most important things to ask is how the clinic manages pain. If the vet doesn't manage pain and still operates on the old theory that "dogs just don't feel pain the way humans do," find another vet.

Veterinarians have to know how to manage pain. Some surgeries, such as orthopedic procedures, are painful during

Can Purebreds Have a Hybrid Vigor?

Yes, purebred dogs can have hybrid vigor when a breeder uses two line outcrosses in a breed. Sometimes purebred breeders will do a lot of line breeding, then use dogs from inbred lines to cross, and that causes the same hybrid vigor that people think only exists in mixed breeds. (An outcross is when a dog and bitch who are unrelated in recent generations are bred to each other; line breeding occurs when a dog and bitch are bred who have common relatives in the past few generations, but not the last two or so; and inbreeding is when a dog and bitch who are closely related in recent generations are bred to each other.) The farther away that you get from common relatives, the healthier the offspring is likely to be.

recuperation, and appropriate pain control affects the healing process. Your dog does not have to endure pain after surgery the way dogs used to a decade ago. In fact, not helping a dog to manage his pain after a procedure is now considered inhumane.

Trust Your Instincts

Trust your instincts when part of it is personal ease: Do you like the vet? Does the vet explain things well and look you in the eye, or does she make you feel rushed and not let you finish mentioning your concerns?

Look at Location and Hours

Next, look at the clinic's location and hours. Does it offer urgent care after hours if you have an emergency? If you have an emergency, where else and how far are you expected to go?

Check for Extra Services

Do you need other services? Does the clinic board or groom dogs? Does it have a network of specialists with which it works on a regular basis, or on staff? If you feed a raw diet or prefer alternative medicine, find out how the vet feels about it. You don't want to end up arguing with your vet over something that you believe in. Your life will be easier if you work with someone who agrees with your approach.

Your mix depends on you to keep him healthy.

Visit Your Favorite Clinics

Select your top two clinics and visit them. See how the staff interacts with you, and watch how they handle animals in the lobby. Ask for a tour of the clinic.

Meeting the Veterinarian

Whenever a new dog joins your household, whether a puppy or an adult, that dog should see the vet within a few days of his arrival to establish a relationship, have a file made, and receive an exam to see if he has any medical condition(s) that you need to know about. A baseline physical exam can be helpful down the road. Bring a fecal sample to this appointment so that the vet can look

for nutrition-stealing worms. If your dog isn't altered, schedule an appointment for that as long as the vet determines that no other medical priorities exist.

Bringing in Baby

If your wee new puppy has never been to the vet before, consider a get-to-know you visit to the clinic. A get-to-know-you visit specifically does not include anything that the puppy would consider "unpleasant," such as shots or rectal temperature taking. Ask the vet to place your puppy onto the exam table and just fuss over him and give him treats. You want her to do this so that your puppy's first experience at the vet does not make him afraid of vet visits for the rest of his life. That first visit is the most critical to shape his attitude about going to the vet; it is in no way a waste of money or time. If the first visit involves vaccines, a rectal thermometer, and having his toenails trimmed, he is more likely to dislike going. For the price of an office visit and a little time, you will have an easier time getting your dog to the vet. Do whatever you can to make sure that he doesn't have good cause to hate going to the clinic!

Annual Physical Exams

At an annual physical exam, the veterinarian will run her hands all over your dog. She'll touch his stomach to make sure that it feels normal; listen to his heart and lungs; inspect his skin for lumps and bumps; check that his eyes, ears, and teeth look normal; and observe how he walks and moves. The vet will weigh your dog as well.

Throughout his life, your dog should have annual exams, although old dogs really need a physical examination twice a year. For your beloved senior, regular blood tests can check for problems with organ function (kidneys, liver, etc.). As with humans, diseases are most treatable when they are new and have not yet taken hold.

VACCINATIONS: A CONTROVERSIAL TOPIC

Over the past few years, as health issues have appeared to crop up from the administration of vaccines, vaccination schedules have become somewhat controversial. Everyone used to believe that vaccines couldn't hurt, but people now realize that that's not always correct, and the "less is more" theory has become popular. Keep in mind, though, that the vast majority of dogs have no problems whatsoever with vaccines. Currently, however, some veterinarians and owners feel that overuse of vaccines is related to the increase of autoimmune diseases.

The bottom line is that each dog has an individual reaction to vaccines, and one schedule will not fit every dog. Annual vaccinations for most vaccines are unnecessary; in fact, some vaccines don't even protect for a full year. Vaccines should be looked at as a benefit-versus-risk situation, and you and your vet are the ones who must decide what is best for your dog. Your veterinarian can help you personalize the vaccine protocol to your dog's particular risks, which spring from considerations such as geography and activities. For example, if your dog participates in performance events or works with a lot of other dogs on a regular basis in such avenues as search and rescue, it's best to lean toward more vaccinations. If you do not live in an area where Lyme disease is a factor, then there is no need to consider the Lyme vaccine. The decisions on which you base your vaccination schedule boil down to common sense.

Having a vet you trust is critical.

Then Why Does My Puppy Need so Many Vaccinations?

Puppies present special considerations. They are born protected by their mother's antibodies, although those maternal antibodies don't last long. Nonetheless, puppies have immature, or rather inexperienced, immune systems. *Antibodies* are the part of the dog's immune system that protect him from disease. Technically, the body produces antibodies as a response to foreign substances called *antigens*; the antibodies neutralize the antigens. Your puppy must be exposed to antigens for him to produce antibodies on his own. After he is exposed to antigens, he can create his own antibodies.

A puppy's maternal antibodies negate any vaccinations that he gets because antibodies find the vaccine and kill it; that is exactly what antibodies are meant to do. This means that your puppy's immune system is working. It also means that you have to wait for the mother's antibodies to be gone from a puppy's body before any vaccinations are effective. To complicate the situation, maternal antibodies for specific diseases fade at different times, which is why puppies need a series of vaccinations instead of just getting them all in one visit.

Vaccination Schedule

The American Animal Hospital Association (AAHA) has recommendations for vaccination schedules: the puppy series for core vaccines, a booster for adults at one year, and boosters every three years thereafter. These are considered the core of any vaccination schedule. Note that some vaccinations, such as bordetella, are not considered necessary for every dog.

The Puppy Series

Puppy vaccinations begin with the four-in-one combination shot plus a separate rabies vaccine. The four-in-one, called DHPP, includes distemper, hepatitis, parainfluenza, and parvovirus. Puppies who do not have this series are prone to any of these diseases. Whether or not you choose to vaccinate regularly after your dog is an adult is one thing, but for a good "shot" at a healthy life, your puppy must have this basic series.

Optional

As mentioned earlier, some vaccinations are optional and depend on your geographic location and lifestyle. Does your dog walk in the woods every day? Does he participate in competitive agility trials or take obedience classes regularly? Do you live in the city, where walked dogs all do their business on the same cement sidewalks?

Bordetella Vaccine

If your dog has contact with a lot of dogs, such as at shows or in a boarding kennel, he should have a bordetella vaccination. Bordetella is a bacteria that causes kennel cough, a highly contagious respiratory disease similar to a cold. It is sometimes associated with the parainfluenza virus. Most often it goes away on its own, just like a human cold, but sometimes antibiotics are needed.

Titers

Some people like to test their dog's blood for titer levels of vaccinations. A *titer* is the measure or number of antibodies that a dog has against a given virus. A blood test can determine titer levels. However, what those levels actually mean in terms of whether you should give boosters is a bit controversial right now. Some veterinarians believe that you should not give more boosters if the titers are sufficient to protect against disease, and others believe that boosters should be given no matter what.

The tests cost more than the vaccinations, but some people do it because they prefer spending the money rather than vaccinating unnecessarily.

Giardia Vaccine

Most veterinarians typically do not recommend the giardia vaccine, because unfortunately, it does not prevent the dog from getting giardia. However, it does lessen the physical symptoms of the disease.

Lyme Disease Vaccine

Lyme disease vaccination is only recommended if your dog lives, or often visits, areas with deer ticks. Ask your veterinarian whether deer ticks live in your area.

Why Vaccinate With Boosters After the Initial Series?

Before you decide against ever vaccinating for anything other than rabies after the initial puppy series, remember that very few dogs have reactions to or problems with vaccines unless they have an autoimmune problem. The chances of a problem occurring as a result of a vaccination are still statistically small.

Take into account that vaccination was responsible for ending

Make sure that your puppy receives his basic puppy series of vaccinations.

the epidemic of canine parvovirus, a disease that veterinarians first saw in the 1970s and that is common without vaccination. Because so many people vaccinate their pets for rabies, almost all cases of rabies in the United States are associated with wildlife, notably bats and raccoons.

Use common sense and your veterinarian's guidance: If your dog has autoimmune problems or another existing disease, either wait to vaccinate or don't do it all. If your dog is otherwise healthy, the AAHA's recommended vaccination schedule is a reasonable guide.

Vaccination Schedule

Disease	Description	Vaccination Schedule
Distemper	An airborne viral disease of the lungs and intestines	Administer one dose at 6–8 weeks, 9–11 weeks, and 12–14 weeks of age
Hepatitis	A viral disease that affects the liver	Administer one dose at 6–8 weeks, 9–11 weeks, 12–14 weeks of age
Parainfluenza	The canine equivalent of infectious bronchitis	Administer one dose at 6–8 weeks, 9–11 weeks, and 12–14 weeks of age
Parvovirus	A viral disease that affects the intestines	Administer one dose at 6–8 weeks, 9–11 weeks, and 12–14 weeks of age
Rabies	A viral disease of the central nervous system	Administer one dose as early as 3 months of age

NEUTERING YOUR MIXED BREED

Some people are squeamish at the thought of altering their dog (some because it sounds uncomfortable, unmanly, or expensive) but really, other than vaccinations, there isn't a single thing that you can do that will ensure good health as much as altering. It will also reduce some behavioral problems that are related to hormones (notably aggression and wandering seen in males). Veterinarians recommend that dogs be neutered any time after eight weeks of age.

Too many unwanted dogs are euthanized each year because there aren't enough good homes for them all. The need for this terrible process could be eliminated if family pets were altered; it's the classic "a stitch in time saves nine."

Females

A spay involves removing both ovaries and the uterus. It is

major surgery but so common that it is one of the first surgeries taught to veterinary students. If your female is spayed before her first heat, she has almost no possibility of developing mammary cancer. If she is spayed after her first heat, there is a 7 percent chance that she will develop it. If you wait until after her second heat, she has a one in four chance of developing it. Mammary cancer can be localized and relatively easy to deal with, or it can be fatal—but no matter what, spaying is the only preventive measure that you can take. It also means that you won't have to deal with the mess and upheaval of the household's male canines when a bitch goes into heat. (*Heat* is the period of time in which the bitch is ready to mate, and all the males around know it.)

Another reason to spay is that after being in heat, bitches can get pyometra, a life-threatening infection of the uterus. This infection usually occurs in middle-aged to older bitches in the six weeks after heat. A hormone, progesterone, causes the blood-filled uterine lining to multiply; the progesterone also lowers immune function within the uterus so that vaginal bacteria can get into the uterus more easily and cause infection. During pyometra, the uterus swells extensively because it is filled with pus, bacteria, dying or dead tissue, and toxins. The treatment is to spay her immediately, otherwise, the infection is fatal. Pyometra is quite common in older unspayed females. It's considered something that *will* happen sooner or later, not something that *could* happen. Bitches have no equivalent to menopause and will have heat cycles their entire lives, so the risk exists as long as they are alive.

Males

Males receive both behavioral and medical benefits from neutering. The behavioral changes are those influenced by testosterone; it doesn't mean that he is suddenly going to answer your recall command when he never did before. The changes lessen his interest in roaming; 90 percent of neutered dogs don't roam afterward. The change in testosterone also lessens aggressive behavior toward other male dogs in about 60 percent of them. In addition, urine marking is eliminated in 50 percent of neutered dogs, and inappropriate mounting is eliminated in 70 percent. Don't buy into any old myths—your dog will not become lethargic or gain weight as a result of being neutered.

Why Your Dog Needs a Regular Rabies Vaccination

A rabies vaccination is legally required in every state because the deadly rabies disease can be transmitted from dogs to people; it is so deadly that, by the time symptoms appear one to three months after infection, it is too late for either a dog or a human to survive.

American people and dogs typically get rabies after being bitten by a rabid animal. Any mammal can get rabies. According to the United States Centers for Disease Control and Prevention (CDC), "Wild animals are much more likely to carry rabies, especially raccoons, skunks, bats, foxes, and coyotes. However, dogs, cats, cattle (cows), or any warm-blooded animal can pass rabies to people. People usually get rabies from the bite of an infected animal." The CDC also states that "cats, cattle, and dogs are the most frequently reported rabid domestic animals in the United States."

Most municipalities require proof of rabies vaccinations to issue a dog license.

The prostate gland enjoys far better health in neutered dogs than in intact ones. If the testosterone level isn't reduced, the prostate gland gradually enlarges with age. At some point, your senior dog will have an uncomfortable prostate; a few have problems defecating because of it. Also, a neutered dog is less likely to have prostate infections, which are not likely to clear up without neutering.

PARASITES

Several types of harmful parasites exist, including fleas, ticks, and worms. The problems that these parasites create range from minor to major. While prevention is easiest, it's not always possible, and if you do find yourself in the midst of a parasite problem, the sooner they are eliminated, the better off your dog will be. Thankfully, most parasites have a short life cycle, but getting rid of them can still feel like waging a war!

Fleas

Fleas are the most common parasite that affects dogs. These little bloodsuckers can make your pet anemic if the infestation is severe enough. Certainly, it takes a large number of fleas to make a dog anemic, but it's hardly unusual; some dogs end up needing blood transfusions to treat their anemia. Far more common, however, is an allergy to fleas, which can make your dog absolutely miserable. Even if a dog isn't allergic to fleas (and that is one of the most common of all canine allergies), their bites still itch. There's a reason that fleas are called pests!

Fleas are notoriously indiscriminate when it comes to selecting a host; in fact, they're fond of most mammals. You and your dog could be walking along, enjoying the day, when a bunch of fleas jump up and bite. Be grateful that fleas can't fly; it's bad enough that they can jump so high.

The Flea Life Cycle

Disgusting as the flea's life cycle is (it seems that they spend their lifetimes mooching off the environment without doing any work to pay the rent), it helps to understand what it is so that you can disrupt it. Adult female fleas lay eggs on dogs, and the eggs fall off and hatch where they land. When the time is right, flea larvae are released, and they feed on organic material. Then the larvae develop into pupae, a state in which they can remain dormant for a while. The pupae then hatch into adult fleas, who, like vampires, look for a host to suck blood from. After they feed off their unwilling host, the new adult females lay eggs and the cycle begins again. The only way to get rid of fleas is to break the life cycle.

Symptoms

A flea can park on a host for quite a while, and its saliva can irritate a dog's skin. Dogs who are allergic to fleas have what is called *flea dermatitis*; scratching at the bites irritates the skin more than the flea bite did. Thus, the skin itself is irritated more by the dog than the flea. "Corncob nibbling" is a telltale sign of fleas, in addition to licking, chewing, and biting at the skin. If your dog is allergic to fleas, he can be treated with corticosteroids, such as prednisone, to ease the inflammation and itching.

Neuter your mixed breed—it's best for his health and cuts down on dog overpopulation.

How to Control Fleas

Flea control has changed drastically in the last decade. Most over-the-counter products are ineffective or far less effective than the medications your veterinarian can prescribe. If you select a product that only kills adults, you are merely eliminating 1 to 5 percent of the fleas at any given time, and all too soon some new adults will have matured. With this in mind, make sure that your flea control product is an insect growth regulator, because if you only kill the adult fleas, you're not going to get rid of the problem.

Some methods for getting rid of fleas are generally ineffective because they have developed an immunity to the primary ingredient, which is usually permethrin. Bathing with a flea shampoo and using a flea dip, flea spray, or flea collar are all far less effective than today's new medications, and none of these older methods is waterproof.

The best flea control methods are medications available from your veterinarian, typically a topical liquid that is applied between the shoulder blades. These are effective for about a month and continually kill fleas that mature into adulthood. Ask your veterinarian for help in selecting the best product for your dog's situation because some are better for certain situations than others. Some products have age minimums or cannot be used in pregnant or nursing dogs. Flea preventives must be carefully selected for sick, immune-compromised, or underweight dogs.

The first step should be to use a topical adulticide or a systemic drug. These medications are available by prescription only. Some breeds are overly sensitive to these medications, so unless your veterinarian says otherwise, only use one of these products at a time.

Fleas are found on most mammals.

Cleaning the house and treating the yard can help. If you have an extremely bad infestation, and the fleas have moved on to your ankles, consider a professional exterminator. Even without professional help, you can fog areas in the house, vacuum frequently, wash bedding in hot water (warm water doesn't kill anything), and mop hard floors. For your yard, powders, sprays, and microscopic parasitic nematodes are available. Shady areas in your yard should definitely be treated. A good yard spray that contains diazinon and is approved for flea control is effective, but the yard has to be treated weekly for four weeks to break the flea life cycle. In hot and humid climates, flea season is all year long. In seasonal climates, begin flea control around May or June.

Ticks

Ticks suck blood. They can transmit some unpleasant if not downright dangerous diseases, including babesiosis, Rocky Mountain spotted fever, ehrlichiosis and Lyme disease. Babesiosis causes red blood cell destruction and anemia. Rocky Mountain spotted fever can cause heart inflammation, internal hemorrhage, and organ failure. Ehrlichiosis harms bone marrow activity and causes inflammation and organ damage. Lyme disease causes arthritis signs, fever, and the potential for kidney disease. While a diagnosis of Lyme disease is frightening to anyone, it's easier to treat in dogs than in people, although it takes a long time.

Like mites and scorpions, ticks are eight-legged arthropods. (Fleas are insects, not arthropods.) Ticks can transmit diseases when they suck blood. If well fed first, these bloodsuckers can go for months without eating. Ticks also can cause a type of neurotoxin-induced paralysis in dogs five to nine days after they are bitten. However, as long as the dog survives the acute bite, no long-term complications occur.

Ticks do not jump or fly—they crawl or drop down. They are attracted to motion, light patterns, warmth, odors that indicate that people are close by, and the carbon dioxide that you and your dog exhale. Ticks climb onto tall objects like a tree or fence and patiently wait for a mammal to cruise by; then, they jump down from their height onto the mammal. Because it doesn't hurt when ticks bite, most people and dogs don't notice. A bite can become infected, though, so check both yourself and your dog when you come back in from an area likely to have ticks.

Cats and Flea Control Products

Never use any dog flea control products on a cat. A cat's nervous system is far more sensitive than a dog's, and using products labeled for dogs, even if you've adjusted for weight, can kill cats. Also, if your dog and cat sleep together or snuggle up a lot, don't use anything containing permethrin on the dog because cats react badly—potentially fatally— to this ingredient.

Prevention

Ticks are disgusting and dangerous, not to mention hardy, so get ticked off enough that you carry out prevention. Many products help to prevent ticks, such as acaricide collars and spot treatments. Your choice should depend on your geographic area and your dog's age. Some of these preventives can be used on puppies, and some cannot. As with flea products, don't use more than one preventive at a time. Do not use spray insecticides that are made for use on clothing on your pet.

Also, avoid walking in the woods during prime flea and tick season in warm weather. Keep grass and weeds short as well.

Worms

Dogs can get several types of worms, including heartworms, hookworms, roundworms, tapeworms, and whipworms. Most worms absorb digested food through their skin as it floats by in the intestines. Some worms travel a bit within the body, but at some point in their life cycle they arrive in the intestines, which is why a vet will examine a fecal sample to look for these parasites. Your veterinarian can deworm your dog with medication.

Heartworms

Heartworms live in the heart and pulmonary arteries of an infected dog. The worms take up too much space in the heart so that less blood is pumped. The arteries dilate, and eventually, aneurysms and blood clots, or *embolisms*, result.

The life cycle of a heartworm is quite interesting. Adult female heartworms (which can grow to 14 inches [36 cm] in length) birth their live young into their host's bloodstream. The young are called *microfilariae*. When biting an infected animal for a blood meal, mosquitoes become infected with these young worms. In two weeks, the microfilariae are able to infect a canine host. When the mosquito bites a dog, the infective larvae enter the dog through the bite wound. In about six months, the larvae mature into adult worms. Adult heartworms can live for five to seven years in a dog.

The first sign of heartworm infection is a cough, then exercise intolerance, and then abnormal lung sounds. The signs can progress to difficulty breathing, temporary loss of consciousness because of poor blood flow to the brain, an enlarged liver, fluid buildup in the stomach, and abnormal heart sounds.

Heartworm treatment is potentially fatal. The drug used is an arsenic derivative; it's not only hard on the dog, it's painful. Some dogs feel okay after the two injections (for which they are generally hospitalized in case of an adverse reaction), but some are in pain for days because the needle used for delivery is large and inserted in both sides of the lumbar area. After the final treatment, the dog must be strictly confined for about six weeks. Any exercise, including going for a walk, can cause a fatal embolism (clot).

Thus, prevention is far easier on you and your dog than is treatment. Ask your vet if your dog should be on a preventive year round; this may depend on the area in which you live. Most people who follow holistic or alternative medicine and may avoid Western

How to Remove a Tick

If you find a tick on your dog, get it out right away, because if it's taken off within 24 hours, you can prevent disease transmission. (Cats are pretty efficient at removing ticks from themselves but not from their canine housemates.) For your safety, dab rubbing alcohol on the tick, use tweezers to take hold of it, and pull on the tick gently. Try not to leave the head embedded or squeeze the tick. Sometimes ticks survive being tossed down the toilet or sink, so drop the removed tick into alcohol or insecticide to make sure that you've killed it. Some out-of-date methods of removal, such as hot matches or petroleum jelly, not only don't work but allow the tick to stay attached for a longer period.

medications, still use a preventive because heartworm treatment is so hard on dogs.

Hookworms

Hookworms can take a significant amount of blood from a dog. Adults clamp down six sharp teeth that resemble hooks into an intestinal wall and drink a lot of blood. Described as "voracious," their bite is so bad that the wall can still bleed after the worm has disengaged. In acute cases, dogs are hospitalized for fluid and blood transfusions. The problems tend to be acute in puppies and chronic in adults. Hookworms are nothing to fool around with. They mate and live in the small intestine, and they are passed out with feces. It's hard to get rid of hookworms if both eggs and larvae are in the small intestine.

Check your dog for ticks after he's been outside.

Signs of infestation include pale mucous membranes (check for pale gums); tarry feces or diarrhea; lack of appetite; cough; and even sudden death from blood loss. Puppies are more likely to die from blood loss than adult dogs.

Your veterinarian will select the appropriate deworming medication. Hookworms can be transmitted to unborn puppies as well as to people, but you can prevent the former with appropriate deworming under a veterinarian's care. Puppies who live in a place with a history of hookworm infections should be routinely treated with a dewormer at two-week intervals until they are weaned.

Roundworms

A wandering worm, *Toxocara canis* travels during its life cycle. Dogs, in one of their most unpleasant habits, eat the eggs when ingesting other canines' feces, and the eggs hatch in the dog's intestinal tract. The egg migrates from the intestinal tract to other body tissues; in dogs, the larvae like the liver but move on to the lungs, where they can cause pneumonia. When the larvae move into the upper airways, the dog coughs. The coughing passes the third-stage larvae into the throat. From his throat, the dog swallows the larvae, and it goes back to the intestines. In pregnant dogs, the second-stage larvae do not move to the lungs but instead go to the uterus and the unborn puppies. The larvae then develop into third-stage larvae in the puppies' lungs instead of in the mother's. (Roundworms are more likely to affect puppies than adults, and sometimes they affect entire litters.)

Once the third-stage larvae have returned to the intestine, they mature into fourth-stage larvae and mate in about a week. The entire life cycle only takes about four or five weeks after infection first occurred. The worms can grow to around 7 inches (18 cm) long.

Affected dogs will cough, exhibit a bloated stomach, and have a poor appetite.

When a dog is dewormed, only the worms in the intestine are killed, which accounts for only one part of the life cycle. The vet will deworm three or four times to get all the worms in every stage. Dogs can be treated with an adulticide/larvicide anthelmintic. In severe cases, a dog may need to be hospitalized to receive intravenous fluids.

Tapeworms

In the small intestine, the adult tapeworm *Dipylidium caninum* grabs onto a wall with a hook-like apparatus. To stay secure, it also uses six rows of teeth. Although the length of the adult tapeworm is about 6 inches (15 cm), you only will see small portions of it. The white segments are flat and look like tape; that's how they got their creative name. Once the worm attaches itself, it grows a long tail in several segments. Each segment has an independent digestive system and reproductive tract. As new tail segments form, the older ones move closer to the end of the tail, and then when they get to the tip of the tail, they become disconnected and fall off. By the time a segment gets to the tip of the tail, the only part that remains is the reproductive tract. Thus, when it drops off, it drops a bag of eggs. That bag is then passed out of the body with feces. Once outside the body, the bag breaks open and the tapeworm eggs spread.

And guess what? Larval fleas eat tapeworm eggs! While the larval flea grows, so does the tapeworm it has eaten, so the parasite has a parasite. As the flea sucks blood, it is sometimes licked up and ingested by its host. (You know that dogs will eat anything!) So while the flea corpse cruises through a dog's digestive system, the tapeworm becomes released, and—you guessed it—attaches itself to the intestinal wall. Voila! The life cycle starts all over.

The only way that a dog can get tapeworms is from eating fleas. He doesn't just get them from licking fleas from his own body; he also may ingest them when he kills and eats little critters, such as rodents or rabbits.

Tapeworms can't really hurt your dog, even though they steal a few calories and nutrients. Your dog won't appear sick. The only thing that you will notice are little white things that look like rice or maggots in his feces.

Your vet can deworm your dog with medication.

Fecal tests are not always reliable because the bag of tapeworm eggs has to break apart in the piece of feces being tested. Thus, you can find several worm-free samples, but that doesn't mean that the dog doesn't have worms. You can sometimes see the flat segments near a dog's anus or in his feces.

The only way to prevent tapeworms is to get rid of fleas and control the population. Treatment is a vet-prescribed deworming medication; often, a dog will need a second treatment with the dewormer three weeks later. The good news is that nothing bad happens to your dog because of most adult tapeworms, other than maybe a little rectal itching. There are some tapeworm larvae, though, that can infect the dog's peritoneal cavity.

Whipworms

Dogs get *Trichuris vulpis* by eating whipworm eggs in contaminated soil; it's almost impossible to get them out of affected soil. The whipworm that affects dogs is a tiny bloodsucker. The skinny end is the digestive part, and the fat part is the reproductive end. Together, the skinny and fat ends resemble a whip shape.

Whipworms live in a dog's cecum, the point at which the large intestine meets the small intestine. They lay eggs in the large intestine, and those eggs end up passing out of the body with the

Fever

A dog's normal body temperature ranges from 101° to 102.5°F (38.3° to 39.2°C). If you suspect that your dog has a fever (dogs with fevers tend to be lethargic, and they shiver noticeably), take his temperature rectally with a digital thermometer or with a special veterinary thermometer designed for the ears, although most pet owners are more accurate with the rectal thermometer. Put petroleum jelly on the tip of the thermometer before inserting it 1 or 2 inches (2.5 or 5 cm). Any temperature above 106°F (41.1°C) is life threatening.

If the temperature gets above 105°F (40.6°C), mix half water and half rubbing alcohol together, apply to a washcloth or sponge, and sponge it on your dog. It helps to have a fan blowing on his body while you do this. Apply a cool pack or water compress on top of his head to protect his brain from getting too hot. If he will, let him drink a bit of water, a little at a time, but don't push it if he won't. Discontinue all of this once his temperature lowers to 103°F (39.4°C). You don't want to overdo it.

Do not give ibuprofen or any other drug to your dog without checking with your vet first, because many drugs that humans take for aches, pains, and fever are poisonous to dogs.

dog's feces.

An infestation of whipworms can cause blood-tinged diarrhea because the large intestine becomes inflamed. There isn't enough blood loss from the tiny whipworm to be a problem, but the diarrhea can become chronic. Whipworms can be a problem for a dog with a compromised immune system, but they aren't really an issue for a healthy dog with a normal immune system.

Deworm with medication from your veterinarian; you have to use a specific dewormer, because some of the medications for other worms don't get rid of whipworms. Often, the dog has to be treated again after a month. Have fecal exams performed periodically to make sure that the whipworms are no longer present.

COMMON HEALTH ISSUES

In a breed book, you will read about the genetic diseases that pertain to one breed. Given that mixed breeds could be predisposed to any hereditary disease, it would take a veterinary textbook to discuss all the diseases that could be considered genetic. Instead, the discussion that follows is for some of the more common reasons that dogs go to the veterinarian.

Allergies

An allergy is an exaggerated response of the body to an antigen. Allergies cause the body to overreact to certain substances. The most common allergies that dogs suffer from are food allergies (typically caused by beef, chicken, pork, corn, wheat, or soy), contact allergies, inhalant allergies, and flea allergies. Dogs also may experience secondary infections that can result from scratching and chewing at itchy skin caused by the allergic reaction.

Symptoms

Allergies in dogs don't typically result in sniffing and sneezing as they do in humans, although in rare cases, that can happen. Instead, dogs get reactions in their skin. They can get so itchy that they scratch all the time, causing staph infections in the skin or open wounds. Affected areas are usually red in color and exhibit some level of hair loss. Sometimes allergies show up as recurring skin or ear infections. Any way you look at it, allergies can make both your life and your dog's life miserable.

Treatment

Sadly, there is no cure for allergies, and affected dogs usually have them for life, although medical treatment can lessen the severity. Steroids, particularly prednisone, are used to stop itching. Unfortunately, if the underlying cause of the allergy isn't treated, the itching will always return. Also, using steroids over long periods of time can create other health problems, so it's best to find out what the specific issue is and treat it rather than just generically addressing the issue with steroids. Severely affected dogs can be skin tested, just like humans, and specific hyposensitization medication can be formulated to control the itching without relying on long-term steroid use.

Cancer

Cancer is an uncontrolled growth of abnormal cells. While most cancer can't be prevented, some types can be; for example, spaying a female dog before her first heat significantly reduces the incidence of mammary gland cancer. The most common cancers in dogs are skin tumors, mammary gland (breast) cancer, head and neck cancer, lymphoma, testicular cancer, abdominal cancer, and bone cancer. Some cancers are relatively straightforward enough that your veterinarian can treat them; some are more complex, and for those types, you should consult a

Exercise can help to keep your dog healthy.

veterinary oncologist.

About half of senior dogs get some type of cancer; it is the leading cause of death in dogs over the age of 10 years. Some of these cases are fairly minor and easily treated, and some are not so simple. Often, a tumor is benign, but even benign tumors can have consequences, especially if they are located in an organ. Nonetheless, take heart. Cancer is not always fatal, and treatments are becoming more effective all the time.

Symptoms

According to the American Veterinary Medical Association (AVMA), common signs of cancer in pets are:
- Abnormal swellings that persist or continue to grow
- Bleeding or discharge from any body opening
- Difficulty breathing, urinating, or defecating
- Difficulty eating or swallowing
- Hesitation to exercise or loss of stamina
- Loss of appetite
- Offensive odor
- Persistent lameness or stiffness
- Sores that don't heal
- Weight loss

Treatment

Treatment options usually include surgery, chemotherapy, and radiation. Some cancers respond to just one type, while others require a combination. Mammary gland cancer is often localized and can be treated with one surgery. Some cancers, such as anal sac cancers, often require surgery, chemotherapy, and radiation.

The typical goal in canine cancer treatment is to extend the dog's life; sometimes it "just" buys time and only sometimes provides a cure. In some cases, early detection or lack thereof will determine the outcome. Before you begin cancer treatment, make sure that you understand what the veterinarian expects the treatment to accomplish.

Multi-modality treatment is expensive and sometimes difficult for the dog. If you don't feel that it's worth it to put your dog through this at such an expense to buy only a little time, don't begin treatment. On the other hand, some cancer treatment is simple and only involves surgically removing a tumor.

The diagnosis of any type of cancer is frightening, but new drugs and techniques are always cropping up, and what your particular dog needs may be far easier to accomplish than you assume.

Cataracts

A cataract is an opaque spot in the normally transparent lens of the eye; it can affect either a part of the lens or all of it, but either way the patient can't see through the opacity. Tiny opaque spots don't affect the dog's vision very much, but most opacities keep growing and eventually cause blindness when they grow large enough to block out all light rays to the eyes.

Congenital cataracts, those present at birth, are inherited. Cataracts are also common in diabetic dogs, but those are not congenital.

Call your vet if you notice a change in your dog's behavior.

Symptoms

Signs of cataracts include a whitish look to the eye from the opacity and some level of blindness that may not even be noticeable to a dog owner until the dog is almost entirely blind.

Treatment

Cataracts don't have to be treated; dogs adapt to blindness much better than people do, and unlike glaucoma, pain is not an issue. Cataracts can only be removed surgically, and this is not usually an option unless the veterinarian feels that surgery can restore vision. If the retina is diseased, vision cannot be restored.

If the vet decides on surgery, she will remove the lens capsule. Then, ultrasonic waves bombard the lens to break it up, and the cataract particles are drawn out. The lens can be replaced with an artificial one that allows sharper vision than the dog would otherwise have without a lens. While most dogs see much better with the artificial lens, they still see better without the bad lens than they did with it, and inserting a new lens is an expensive option only done at a client's request. Without a lens implant, post-surgical dogs see objects in reverse—like looking in a mirror—but

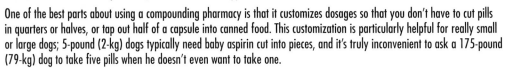

Compounding Pharmacies

Some dogs who eat as though they had an iron stomach will balk at pills, carefully eating around them in kibble or licking off all the peanut butter before spitting them out. If your dog is one of these uncooperative pets who needs to take medicine, a compounding pharmacy can provide a tasty treat for him and relief for you. These pharmacies compound a veterinary medication into something that your dog will actually ingest.

Flavors used most often are chicken, beef, peanut butter, salmon, tuna, and liver. Depending on what medication your dog needs, you could end up with capsules, liquids, tablets, or chews. Sometimes you have a choice of whatever you want, but sometimes the type of medication eliminates certain choices.

One of the best parts about using a compounding pharmacy is that it customizes dosages so that you don't have to cut pills in quarters or halves, or tap out half of a capsule into canned food. This customization is particularly helpful for really small or large dogs; 5-pound (2-kg) dogs typically need baby aspirin cut into pieces, and it's truly inconvenient to ask a 175-pound (79-kg) dog to take five pills when he doesn't even want to take one.

they will see. If the cataract is too advanced, the lens cannot be replaced.

Dogs with cataracts caused by heredity or diabetes have a good prognosis.

Dental Issues

Dental disease occurs when bacteria damages the attachment of the gums to the teeth, the bone is destroyed, and the tooth falls out. If plaque isn't brushed away regularly, the mineral salts in saliva cause tartar. Tartar inflames the gums, and then bacterial organisms start to grow, which cause more gum inflammation. This, in turn, causes swelling of the gum tissue, which traps more bacteria below the gum line and leads to periodontal disease. Periodontal disease occurs when inflammation of a tooth's support occurs; unlike gingivitis, it involves bone loss. Dogs may need root canals, X-rays, orthodontics, crowns, caps, implants, and periodontal surgery.

Symptoms

Signs of dental disease include bad breath, broken teeth, excessive drooling, reluctance to eat or play with chew toys, chewing only on one side of the mouth, pawing at or rubbing the muzzle/mouth, bleeding from the mouth, loss of symmetry of the muzzle and/or lower jaw, swollen/draining tracts under (or in front of) the eye, sudden change in behavior (aggressive or withdrawn), chronic eye infections or drainage with no exact cause or cure, inability to open or close the mouth, chronic sneezing, discolored teeth, abnormal discharge from the nose, or a growth in the mouth.

Treatment

You can prevent dental disease by brushing your dog's teeth daily. Without regular brushing, significant bacteria, plaque, and tartar can build up and cause all kinds of problems, from infections to gingivitis. At this point, he may require a professional cleaning done under anesthesia. While anesthesia is far advanced from a generation ago, why put your dog through it—and the cost and inconvenience of a surgical date—when it's not necessary?

Gingivitis can be treated with a professional dental cleaning and sometimes with anti-inflammatories and antibiotics. Periodontal disease often calls for surgery.

Diarrhea and Vomiting

Diarrhea and vomiting are a sign of gastroenteritis (upset stomach). They sometimes occur at the same time, although not necessarily simultaneously. This isn't a big deal if it only happens a couple times, but see your veterinarian if it goes on all day, especially if your dog is either very young or very old, because dehydration can occur quickly in these two age groups.

Cancer strikes many older pets, but there are many treatments that can help to stop the disease.

Symptoms

Vomiting or having runny stools once or twice is not a big deal. However, when it occurs repeatedly within a few hours or a day, consider this a symptom that warrants a trip to the vet. Also, soft stools on occasion do not require a trip to the vet, but having liquid stools throughout a day can dehydrate the dog, which can be dangerous. If your dog experiences this, take him to the vet.

Treatment

If the cause is simply something your dog ate (kindly referred to as "dietary indiscretion" rather than "eats like a goat"), it will go away on its own. If it's not dietary indiscretion, it is mostly likely a sign of an underlying disease or a case of poison; in either of these cases, get to the veterinarian immediately.

Don't medicate with anything until after you've spoken with your vet, and don't let your dog eat until he has stopped vomiting or passing stools for about six hours. While recuperating, a bland diet is in order, something along the lines of rice.

Ear Infections (Otitis)

The bane of many dog lovers, ear infections are difficult to eradicate. Unlike people, canine ear canals are L-shaped. This shape predisposes dogs to infections because debris, such as earwax, can build up in there, and the ear's L-shape doesn't allow for easy wax removal.

An ear infection usually has an underlying cause. One major trigger is allergies, and the ear infection won't clear up until the source of the allergies is dealt with. Sadly, finding the allergy itself and then eradicating it is not always simple, and that's an understatement. Other causes include foreign bodies (stuff that isn't supposed to be there, like foxtails), ear mites, bacteria, and yeast. The moisture of the wax promotes bacterial growth and infection, and before you know it, there's pus in the ears right along with the wax.

Brushing your mix's teeth will help to avoid many dental problems.

Symptoms

Dogs will show that their ears are uncomfortable by rubbing them on the floor and scratching at them. If your dog has an inner or middle ear infection, which is relatively rare, he may tilt his head and have trouble balancing.

Treatment

Once you know that your dog is

prone to ear infections, you can usually deal with them at home by cleaning the ear canal regularly with an ear-cleaning solution. However, if the trouble persists, an ear flush under general anesthesia can be done, and the contents of the ear can be cultured so that you know exactly what you're dealing with. If the infections are severe enough, surgery can help.

Epilepsy can be managed but not cured.

Epilepsy

Epilepsy is a common neurological syndrome in dogs characterized by recurrent seizures of unknown origin. At first, it can be hard to differentiate them from fainting spells caused by cardiovascular events. After a seizure, dogs are disoriented for a while, either a few minutes or a few hours. Seizures may be caused by something within the brain, such as trauma or infection, or by things outside the brain, such as low blood sugar, trauma, poisons, or hypothyroidism. If a dog is going to have seizures, they usually occur for the first time before he is five years old.

Symptoms

In generalized seizures, dogs typically are unconscious, extend their neck and their legs, and seem to paddle their legs. Some foam at the mouth. They might drool, defecate, or urinate while seizing. While frightening to watch, most seizures are not life threatening.

Treatment

Epilepsy can be managed but not cured. Your vet may prescribe phenobarbital to treat seizures. Generally, treatment with phenobarbital is begun when a dog has more than one seizure a month. Acupuncture has been known to help as well.

Hip Dysplasia

Hip dysplasia is the abnormal development of the hips in which the ball and socket of the hip joint don't fit well together because the ball isn't held in well enough to remain in place. This is a common condition of large dogs; the bigger the dog, the more likely that he has hip dysplasia. Onset occurs during adolescence, but signs might not be noted until the dog is elderly; sometimes, it can occur at any time between those two stages.

The main cause of hip dysplasia is genetic, but nutritional factors (such as trying to get a large-breed dog to grow rapidly into a huge dog by feeding him extra protein or calcium) also can cause it. Responsible breeders know that dogs with hip dysplasia should never be bred, but the problem remains.

Symptoms

Hip dysplasia is usually painful, although it depends on how bad a dog's hips are.

Typically, affected dogs will have problems getting up or do an odd, noticeable "bunny hop" walk.

Treatment

If the hips are bad enough to warrant surgery, different types are available, including a total hip replacement. The choice of which surgery depends on the individual dog's hips. In mild cases, treatment includes keeping the dog comfortable with painkillers and nutritional supplements; treatment is the same as it is for arthritis.

Hypothyroidism

The most common hormone imbalance of dogs, hypothyroidism results from the inadequate production and release of thyroid hormones. In canines, it is most commonly caused by the immune-mediated destruction of the thyroid gland or the natural atrophy of the gland, which is located in the neck near the voice box. It tends to occur in middle-aged or older medium to large dogs.

Symptoms

The signs of hypothyroidism progress slowly but consistently, and the most common ones include hair loss or excessive shedding, lethargy, lack of hair regrowth, dry coat, excessive scaling, hyperpigmentation, recurrent skin infections, mental dullness, weight gain, and intolerance to cold temperatures.

Treatment

Diagnosing this disease can be challenging for a number of reasons; it involves blood tests that measure levels of thyroid hormones. Often, these tests must be repeated. However, treatment is pretty straightforward: pills with thyroid hormone. Treatment is lifelong.

Upset stomachs often occur in dogs; call your vet if the problem persists all day.

Patellar Luxation (Slipped Knees)

Slipped knees, or patellar luxation, is a problem most commonly seen in small dogs in whom the knee joint pops in and out of place. It has a genetic basis, although sometimes it can result from trauma. Veterinarians recognize four stages of progression. Affected breeds and mixes typically include Affenpinschers, Brussels Griffons, Chihuahuas, English Toy Spaniels, Greyhounds, Japanese Spaniels, Maltese, Manchester Terriers, Miniature Pinschers, Papillons, Pekingese, Pomeranians, Poodles, Pugs, Shih Tzu, Silky Terriers, and Yorkshire Terriers.

Symptoms

Symptoms of patellar luxation can be seen by the age of six months. A rear leg appears to lock up, affecting the dog's walk into a kind of skipping gait, and then the knee joint slides back into place and the dog walks normally again. When the patella pops out, the dog skips around to get the joint back into place.

Treatment

No treatment is necessary for mild cases, which can be treated with restricted exercise, weight loss, and aspirin. When the dog can't pop his patella back into place quickly, the situation changes a bit, and surgery is required to prevent painful and permanent

First-Aid Kit

Having a first-aid kit in your home and/or car is practical. You can buy one or make your own. Inside your kit, put in appropriate phone numbers, such as your regular clinic and your emergency hospital, as well as the Poison Control Center for Animals. It's best not to use a human kit for canines, because those contain things that should not be used on dogs, such as ibuprofen.

Basic supplies include:

- Alcohol pads to clean scissors and tweezers—don't use these on a wound
- Antiseptic solution for cleansing wounds
- Eye wash
- First-aid information
- Gauze pads
- Gauze rolls
- Iodine prep solution, an antiseptic solution for cleaning wounds
- Latex gloves for you to wear so that you don't contaminate a wound
- Scissors to cut tape and gauze, and to clip hair around wounds
- Triple antibiotic ointment to promote wound healing
- tweezers
- Vet Wrap, a flexible bandage to wrap around an injury, that sticks to itself without need for tape or clips

Having everything you need in a first-aid kit isn't going to help if you don't know what to do with it. For example, if you wrap vet wrap too tightly, you could accidentally cut off circulation. If you create your own kit or buy one without a guide in it, purchase a guide and keep it in the kit.

lameness. The surgical fix is best done sooner rather than later, because it's easier to repair in an early stage. After surgery, the dog must avoid exercise for a couple of months.

Urinary Tract Infection

A urinary tract infection (UTI) occurs when bacteria get inside the bladder and start to multiply, causing an irritation. Bladder infections are a common cause of urinary incontinence in young adult females.

Symptoms

Signs include drinking far more water than usual, urinating only a little bit at a time, urinating frequently and in multiple spots, an inability to hold urine for as long as usual, or bloody urine.

Treatment

Although frustrating, urinary tract infections are easily diagnosed and treated. A urinalysis can sometimes show bacteria in the urine, but a urine culture will confirm which type of organism is causing the problem and allow the veterinarian to select the best antibiotic for the particular bug.

Your dog will likely feel better within a couple of days of antibiotic treatment. Be sure to administer all of them, or the infection may quickly return. Not finishing the antibiotics is a bit like not making sure that a fire is all the way out.

ALTERNATIVE MEDICINE

Holistic medicine includes such practices as acupuncture, chiropractic, herbal therapy, and homeopathy. There are also related fields, such as shiatsu, Reiki, and others. Some people think that these alternative modalities are useless, while others believe wholeheartedly that they make a positive impact on canine health. Do your research, consult your veterinarian, and act on what you feel is in your dog's best interest.

Hip and joint problems can prohibit your dog from jumping and playing.

If you are uncomfortable with discussions of vital force and energy, think about what can benefit your dog rather than the terminology. It's no secret that Western, or *allopathic* medicine, can't cure every problem, and you may find that alternative medicine can help—or not. As with allopathic medicine, you must find an alternative practitioner who has undergone significant training and who knows what she's doing.

Acupuncture

Acupuncturists stimulate specific points in the body to heal or lessen pain or inflammation.

Many dog owners discover that their dogs get relief from acupuncture that they were unable to find in allopathic medicine. The goal is to stimulate the flow of energy and balance the body.

Acupuncturists treat specific concerns with needles, massage, and heat. The needles are painlessly inserted at specific sites to create a physiologic response. With dogs, it can help with medical problems and some behavioral problems, including fearfulness and compulsive disorders. Acupuncture causes the release of hormones, such as cortisone, and natural painkillers, such as endorphins, and other substances that stimulate tissue to respond and to increase the blood supply to troubled areas.

Most dogs who undergo acupuncture are being treated for chronic health problems, such as pain, arthritis, gastrointestinal disease, respiratory problems, skin conditions, and kidney disease. Most dogs who get acupuncture are geriatrics, and it's also useful for those undergoing chemotherapy.

Chiropractic

Chiropractic can be successfully used with dogs. This modality works on the mechanical causes of disease but does not use medication. A dog's spine has more than 100 joints. When a joint doesn't move correctly, movement is affected. Canine chiropractors seek to remove subluxations (joints in which movement has changed) or fixations (joints that have become immobilized) by gently adjusting the spine or affected joints back into proper alignment.

Depending on the state in which you live, your veterinarian may have to refer you to a chiropractor. Most animal chiropractors are not veterinarians but rather chiropractors certified to work with animals. Some veterinarians are certified in chiropractic care.

Herbs

Herbal remedies use the leaves, roots, bark, flowers, and seeds of plants to promote healing. Although herbal remedies take longer to have an effect than prescription medication, they can be quite effective. As with drugs, some have side effects. If it's strong enough to have a good impact, it's strong enough to have a bad impact, and it can cause side effects. Herbs can work in many positive ways but they must be used cautiously and with the advice of someone familiar with them, so consult an herbalist. Do

AHVMA

To learn more about alternative medicine, visit the American Holistic Veterinary Medical Association (AHVMA) at www.ahvma.org.

not determine which herbs to use or what dosages to give on your own.

Some people think that because a substance is natural, it cannot hurt, but this is a misconception. You must dose properly based on weight to avoid fatalities. Numerous books are available that will help you understand herbal treatment, but always consult with someone who is trained in herbal treatment so that you don't inadvertently, and with the best of intentions, harm your dog.

Homeopathy

The principle on which homeopathy is based is the Law of Similars, in which like cures like. It fights disease with tiny quantities of substances that get the body to fight disease on its own, rather than with medication. Proponents believe that a substance that can cause symptoms of a disease at normal doses can stimulate the body to fight and eradicate those symptoms at tiny doses. To find a veterinarian in your area who practices homeopathy, contact the Academy of Veterinary Homeopathy.

THE AGING MIXED BREED

Mixed-breed dogs age just like purebreds; they get progressively less active, they sleep more, they usually have to see the vet more often, they may not be as interested in food or play, they snore, and often they sprout little skin warts. Hearing and vision may dim, and arthritis is common.

You might want to explore alternative medicine for your mix.

Eating can be a problem because some dogs simply lose a bit of their appetite and might need to be tempted with variety. They will need fewer calories but more good nutrition, so healthy snacks are a better choice than pizza crust, no matter what your dog tells you.

Some dogs may have a certain level of cognitive dysfunction that is a bit similar to Alzheimer's

*Herbal medicine,
acupuncture, and
chiropractic are all
available to your dog.*

disease in people. This is called *canine cognitive dysfunction*. Depending on the color of your dog's coat, you may see a whitening muzzle. Some dogs will get anxious; many will follow loved ones around the house, even if they are still going to the kitchen while their humans are already on their way back. Unless your dog becomes ill, the process of aging will seem very slow, and one day you will realize that there's been a change over the past year that you hadn't even noticed.

Old age is a tremendously satisfying time to share with a dog. The bond you have achieved with your dog is at its deepest, most profound level in these years. Enjoy it!

Euthanasia: The Kindest Gift

As difficult as this subject is to think about, euthanasia is truly the kindest gift that you can provide your dog. It is a quick, painless overdose of anesthesia that causes an animal to become unconscious and then causes his heart to stop beating.

While some animals die naturally, most often the body will outlive a dog's will to continue. You can assist your pet by alleviating his discomfort and pain and by letting him bypass those last few terribly uncomfortable days. In other words, you can control the quality of his death. While everyone has individual opinions on when to do this, most people feel that it is better to do it a day too soon than a day too late because of the amount of discomfort you can eliminate.

Whether or not to be present with your dog is a personal decision. If you feel that you can be strong and not fall apart, you will be a great comfort to your dog. Certainly, dogs prefer to have their people with them for this. It also will help your grieving process if you see how peaceful his passing is. If, however, you feel that you are sure to fall apart, your emotions may make it more difficult not only for your dog but also for the veterinarian. Family histrionics only increase the stress on your dog. If you feel that you may not handle this well, consider asking someone who knows your pet to go with him.

As part of the grieving process, many people cremate their dog and keep the ashes. Some prefer the idea of another type of memorial, such as jewelry engraved with the dog's name;

As your mix ages, increase his vet visits to twice a year.

a figurine urn; a donation to the shelter from which he was adopted or to another humane organization; or a memorial marker in the yard. Thinking about how to memorialize a friend helps most people move through the stages of grief. Eventually, you will arrive at the point at which what you think about most are all the wonderful memories of a lifetime spent together.

Much of good health depends on genetics, over which you have no control. Like purebreds, you can see mixed breeds who are sick off and on for their entire lives or dogs who only go to the veterinarian for annual exams until they're senior citizens. Good nutrition, consistent exercise, veterinary care, mental stimulation, and love and affection all play a part in your dog's health.

ASSOCIATIONS AND ORGANIZATIONS

BREED CLUBS

American Canine Hybrid Club
10509 S & G Circle
Harvey, AR 72841
Telephone: (479) 299-4415
E-mail: ach@achclub.com
www.achclub.com

Crossbreed & Mongrel Club
Mr Jim Colley, Membership Secretary
'Raymar', Welton Road
Nettleham, Lincoln
LN2 2LU
United Kingdom
Telephone: 01522 751576
E-mail: chairperson@
crossbreed-and-mongrel-club.org.uk
www.crossbreed-and-mongrel-club.org.uk/

Mixed Breed Dog Clubs of America (MBDCA)
c/o Linda Lewis-Membership Secretary
13884 State Route 104
Lucasville, OH 45648-8586
Telephone: (740) 259-3941
E-mail: libi-lew@juno.com
www.mbdca.org

North American Mixed Breed Registry (NAMBR)
RR#2 - 8649 Appleby Line
Campbellville, Ontario
Canada L0P 1B0
E-mail: info@nambr.cardoso.ca
www.nambr.cardoso.ca/contact.php

PET SITTERS

National Association of Professional Pet Sitters
15000 Commerce Parkway, Suite C
Mt. Laurel, New Jersey 08054
Telephone: (856) 439-0324
Fax: (856) 439-0525
E-mail: napps@ahint.com
www.petsitters.org

Pet Sitters International
201 East King Street
King, NC 27021-9161
Telephone: (336) 983-9222
Fax: (336) 983-5266
E-mail: info@petsit.com
www.petsit.com

RESCUE ORGANIZATIONS AND ANIMAL WELFARE GROUPS

American Humane Association (AHA)
63 Inverness Drive East
Englewood, CO 80112
Telephone: (303) 792-9900
Fax: 792-5333
www.americanhumane.org

American Society for the Prevention of Cruelty to Animals (ASPCA)
424 E. 92nd Street
New York, NY 10128-6804
Telephone: (212) 876-7700
www.aspca.org

Royal Society for the Prevention of Cruelty to Animals (RSPCA)
Telephone: 0870 3335 999
Fax: 0870 7530 284
www.rspca.org.uk

The Humane Society of the United States (HSUS)
2100 L Street, NW
Washington DC 20037
Telephone: (202) 452-1100
www.hsus.org

SPORTS

American Herding Breed Association (AHBA)
Siouxsan Eisen, AHBA Membership Coordinator
E-mail: siouxsan@ahba-herding.org
www.ahba-herding.org

American Working Terrier Association (AWTA)
Ann Wendland, Recording Secretary
15720 State Highway 16
Capay, CA 95607
Telephone: (530) 796-2278
E-mail: ratracejrt@gvni.com
www.dirt-dog.com/awta

Canine Freestyle Federation, Inc.
Secretary: Brandy Clymire
E-Mail: secretary@canine-freestyle.org
www.canine-freestyle.org

DockDogs
5183 Silver Maple Lane
Medina, Ohio 44256
Phone: (330) 241-4975
www.dockdogs.com
International Agility Link (IAL)
Global Administrator: Steve Drinkwater
E-mail: yunde@powerup.au
www.agiligyclick.com/~ial

RESOURCES

International Disc Dog Handlers' Association (IDDHA)
1690 Julius Bridge Road
Ball Ground, GA 30107
(770) 735-6200
E-mail: idda@aol.com
www.iddha.com

International Weight Pull Association (IWPA)
E-mail: info@iwpa.net
www.iwpa.net

ISDRA Sled Dog Racing
www.isdra.org

New England Drafting & Driving Club, Inc (NEDDC)
Kathleen Walsh (Secretary)
E-mail: secretary@neddc.com
www.neddc.com

North American Dog Agility Council
11522 South Hwy 3
Cataldo, ID 83810
www.nadac.com

North American Flyball Association
www.flyball.org
1400 West Devon Avenue #512
Chicago, IL 6066
800-318-6312

Unified Frisbee Dog Operations (UFO)
info@ufoworldcup.org
www.ufoworldcup.org

United States Dog Agility Association
P.O. Box 850955
Richardson, TX 75085-0955
Telephone: (972) 487-2200
www.usdaa.com

World Canine Freestyle Organization
P.O. Box 350122
Brooklyn, NY 11235-2525
Telephone: (718) 332-8336
www.worldcaninefreestyle.org

THERAPY

Delta Society
875 124th Ave NE, Suite 101
Bellevue, WA 98005
Telephone: (425) 226-7357
Fax: (425) 235-1076
E-mail: info@deltasociety.org
www.deltasociety.org

Therapy Dogs Incorporated
PO Box 5868
Cheyenne, WY 82003
Telephone: (877) 843-7364
E-mail: therdog@sisna.com
www.therapydogs.com

Therapy Dogs International (TDI)
88 Bartley Road
Flanders, NJ 07836
Telephone: (973) 252-9800
Fax: (973) 252-7171
E-mail: tdi@gti.net
www.tdi-dog.org

TRAINING

Association of Pet Dog Trainers (APDT)
150 Executive Center Drive

Box 35
Greenville, SC 29615
Telephone: (800) PET-DOGS
Fax: (864) 331-0767
E-mail: information@apdt.com
www.apdt.com

National Association of Dog Obedience Instructors
PMB 369
729 Grapevine Hwy.
Hurst, TX 76054-2085
www.nadoi.org

VETERINARY AND HEALTH RESOURCES

Academy of Veterinary Homeopathy (AVH)
P.O. Box 9280
Wilmington, DE 19809
Telephone: (866) 652-1590
Fax: (866) 652-1590
E-mail: office@TheAVH.org
www.theavh.org

American Academy of Veterinary Acupuncture (AAVA)
100 Roscommon Drive, Suite 320
Middletown, CT 06457
Telephone: (860) 635-6300
Fax: (860) 635-6400
E-mail: office@aava.org
www.aava.org

American Animal Hospital Association (AAHA)
P.O. Box 150899
Denver, CO 80215-0899
Telephone: (303) 986-2800
Fax: (303) 986-1700
E-mail: info@aahanet.org
www.aahanet.org/index.cfm

American College of Veterinary Internal Medicine (ACVIM)
1997 Wadsworth Blvd., Suite A
Lakewood, CO 80214-5293
Telephone: (800) 245-9081
Fax: (303) 231-0880
Email:ACTVIM@ACVIM.
org
www.acvim.org

American College of Veterinary Ophthalmologists (ACVO)
P.O. Box 1311
Meridian, Idaho 83860
Telephone: (208) 466-7624
Fax: (208) 466-7693
E-mail: office@acvo.com
www.acvo.com

American Holistic Veterinary Medical Association (AHVMA)
2218 Old Emmorton Road
Bel Air, MD 21015
Telephone: (410) 569-0795
Fax: (410) 569-2346
E-mail: office@ahvma.org
www.ahvma.org

American Veterinary Medical Association (AVMA)
1931 North Meacham Road
– Suite 100
Schaumburg, IL 60173
Telephone: (847) 925-8070
Fax: (847) 925-1329
E-mail: avmainfo@avma.org
www.avma.org

ASPCA Animal Poison Control Center
1717 South Philo Road, Suite 36
Urbana, IL 61802
Telephone: (888) 426-4435
www.aspca.org

British Veterinary Association (BVA)
7 Mansfield Street
London
W1G 9NQ
Telephone: 020 7636 6541
Fax: 020 7436 2970
E-mail: bvahq@bva.co.uk
www.bva.co.uk

Canine Eye Registration Foundation (CERF)
VMDB/CERF
1248 Lynn Hall
625 Harrison St.
Purdue University
West Lafayette, IN 47907-2026
Telephone: (765) 494-8179
E-mail: CERF@vmbd.org
www.vmdb.org

Orthopedic Foundation for Animals (OFA)
2300 NE Nifong Blvd
Columbus, Missouri 65201-3856
Telephone: (573) 442-0418
Fax: (573) 875-5073
Email: ofa@offa.org
www.offa.org

PUBLICATIONS

MAGAZINES

Dog & Kennel
Pet Publishing, Inc.
7-L Dundas Circle
Greensboro, NC 27407
Telephone: (336) 292-4272
Fax: (336) 292-4272
E-mail: info@petpublishing.
com
www.dogandkennel.com

Dogs Monthly
Ascot House
High Street, Ascot,
Berkshire SL5 7JG
United Kingdom
Telephone: 0870 730 8433
Fax: 0870 730 8431
E-mail: admin@rtc-
associates.freeserve.co.uk
www.corsini.co.uk/
dogsmonthly

The Bark
2810-8th St.
Berkeley, CA 94710
Telephone: 1-877-227-5639
Fax: 510-704-0933
E-mail: customerservice@
thebark.com
www.thebark.com

ACKNOWLEDGEMENTS

Many thanks go to Joni Freshman, DVM; Chelse Wieland; Patricia McConnell, Ph.D.; Elizabeth Lundgren, DVM; Stephen Zawistowski, Ph.D. of the ASPCA; Kathy Diamond Davis; Wendy Brooks, DVM; PetNet; and Heidi Nicoll Merson. The information these kind folks shared with me was incredibly useful, and I am grateful to all of them.

AUTHOR

Phyllis DeGioia is an award-winning writer who specializes in writing about veterinary information and pets. She owns Woofing Dog Editorial, LLC and is a member of the Dog Writers Association of America. She has been published in numerous pet publications. As editor of www.veterinarypartner.com, she regularly works with veterinarians and pet experts on informative articles for pet owners. She lives in Madison, Wisconsin, with three small mixed-breed dogs—Fred, Ginger, and Clint—all of whom are rescues.

PHOTO CREDITS

Amy Chiara Allen (Shutterstock): 57; BarbaraJH (Shutterstock): 193; Stacey Bates (Shutterstock): 31; Scott Bolster (Shutterstock): 49; Paulette Braun, Pets By Paulette: 32, 59, 61, 64, 74, 86, 99, 102, 110, 127, 129, 141; Joy Brown (Shutterstock): 70, 103; Karla Caspari (Shutterstock): 33; Florea Marius Catalin (Shutterstock): 68; Kenneth Chelette (Shutterstock): 4, 40, 100; DCP (Shutterstock): 166; Dumitrescu Ciprian-Florin (Shutterstock): 123; Kurt De Bruyn (Shutterstock): 17; Digital Multimedia Creations (Shutterstock): 34 (right); ELEN (Shutterstock): 191; Kimberly Hall (Shutterstock): 137; Susan Harris (Shutterstock): 34 (left); Bryan Hilts, Cloud 9 Photos: 150-151, 167; Dee Hunter (Shutterstock): 63; Stepan Jezek (Shutterstock): 97; Natalya Lakhtakia (Shutterstock): 201; Jim Larson (Shutterstock): 152; jon le-bon (Shutterstock): 189; Michael Ledray (Shutterstock): 66; Dwight Lyman (Shutterstock): 192; Christopher Marin (Shutterstock): 30; Milos Markovic (Shutterstock): 14; Chris Mathews (Shutterstock): 112; Patrick McCall (Shutterstock): 114; Sharon Morris (Shutterstock): 125; Christopher Nagy (Shutterstock): 56; Niserin (Shutterstock): 197; iztok noc (Shutterstock): 133, 200; Olgalis (Shutterstock): 195; Lynne Ouchida: 179; Michael Pettigrew (Shutterstock): 145; photobank ch (Shutterstock): 98; Rix Pix (Shutterstock): 11, 28, 72, 126; Gastev Roman (Shutterstock): 6; Sandra Rugina (Shutterstock): 199; Jennifer Sekerka (Shutterstock): 187; John S. Sfondilias (Shutterstock): 81; Anthony Smith (Shutterstock): 94; Fernando Jose Vasconcelos Soares (Shutterstock): 108, 146; Eline Spek: 168; Nick Stubbs (Shutterstock): 43; HTuller (Shutterstock): 71; troy (Shutterstock): 185; April Turner (Shutterstock): 51, 93; John Urban: 55; Lynn Watson (Shutterstock): 171.

All other photos courtesy Isabelle Francais.

Cover photo: Isabelle Francais.